GOOD
INFLUENCE

How to engage influencers
for purpose and profit

PAUL M. KATZ

Commit Media Books

Published by Commit Media Books, New York, USA
A division of Commit Media LLC.

Please feel free to contact the publisher with any inquiries, including licensing rights, at info@goodinfluencebook.com.

First printed in 2023 in the United States of America.
Typeset by Booknook. Printed by Amazon.
Cover Design by Erika Alyana

Identifiers:
ISBN 979-8-9863261-0-8 (Paperback)
ISBN 979-8-9863261-3-9 (Hardcover)
ISBN 979-8-9863261-1-5 (Ebook)
ISBN 979-8-9863261-2-2 (Audiobook)

Distributed by Commit Media Books,
a division of Commit Media LLC.

To the voiceless,
who need a seat at the table, to be heard, and
the sovereignty to affect change.

We are all going to die. We don't know when.
And now is an excellent time to learn the piano.

—Ancient(ish) Buddhist saying

CONTENTS

ACKNOWLEDGMENTS

Nobody has contributed more to the completion of this book than my life partner, Marie Christine Katz, who gave me the space and time to write. Marie Christine displayed infinite patience when listening to my late-night musings and always responded with crystal clear insights. My children, Taliana and Joris, challenged me creatively and pushed me to think through my views to each one's logical conclusion.

My head researcher for the celebrity information in this book was Anita Katz, my mother. At 93, Anita is intellectually sharper and exhibits greater curiosity than most people a quarter of her age. I would also be remiss not to mention my late father, Louis, who always encouraged me to follow my passion, even if he was unsure where I would end up.

I have been fortunate to have had several mentors who have taken an interest in me despite my tendency not to ask for help. During my formative years, my uncle Sir Alexander Samuels taught me to listen, not interrupt, and cultivate patience. When researching a book and in life, this is a valuable lesson that I still strive to apply every day.

For nearly twenty years in the record business, I had the good fortune to work for Clive Calder, the creative and business virtuoso behind Jive Records and Zomba Music Publishing. Clive gave me many incredible learning and life opportunities, including moving from London to New York. Today, some thirty-seven years later, Clive continues to encourage, support, and guide my philanthropic endeavors. I am grateful to be part of his world.

I have worked with many notable artists and actors during my music career. I respect them all and wish I had one iota of their talent. However, the ones I admire the most devote their talent, platform, and organization to doing good. In particular, a shout out to all those I have been involved with during my philanthropic career, especially Angelique Kidjo, Anna Deavere Smith, Archie Panjabi, Donnie McClurkin, John Legend, Kevin Bacon, Mark Ruffalo, Rihanna, Will Smith, Usher, and Ziggy Marley. They and their respective teams consistently do important work that improves people's lives.

Yet despite interacting with celebrities, my heroes are the unsung and unknown folks doing essential philanthropic, relief, international development, and social justice work near and far from home. One influence in particular was Jane Ortner, a schoolteacher who died too young and whose eulogy was a wake-up call for me to do more for others. And, through ELMA Philanthropies, I have the privilege of working with Rick Frechette, a Catholic priest from Connecticut.

When Father Rick went to Haiti thirty-plus years ago, it was to build an orphanage, but seeing the high child mortality rate, he became a doctor instead. Some thirty years after co-founding the now Haitian-run Saint Damien Pediatric Hospital, Father Rick is still in Haiti ministering to those who have the most need. I and so many others are indebted to each and every one of you who gives so much.

This book would not have come about without the opportunities to work on the social impact campaigns that my philanthropic clients, partners, and friends afforded me. I am particularly grateful for the encouragement and faith placed in me by ELMA Philanthropies' Robyn Calder, Ebony Howard, Janet Kleinbaum, Meron Makonnen, Tom McPartland, and Tarik Ward; Rotary's David Alexander and John Hewko; National Trust's African American Cultural Heritage Action Fund's Brent Leggs, Jason Clement, and Brenda Jones; the Skoll Foundation's Phil Collis, Susan Grego, and Jessica Fleuti; and most recently and most recently ALIMA's Charlie Kunzer. Thanks to every one of you.

Several businesses that I work with excel at combining cause and popular culture. Particular praise goes out to Participant Media's founder Jeff Skoll and CEO David Linde, along with Gabe Brakin, the late Diane Weyermann, Christina Kounelias, Robert Kessel, Anikah Mclaren, Holly Gordon, and Jeannine Tang. They create compelling entertainment on crucial issues, and through impact campaigns achieve positive social change. I am honored to be on the board of Made in Memphis Entertainment. Founders, music icon David Porter and serial entrepreneur Tony Alexander make music their vehicle to give economic and life opportunities to their Memphis community and beyond. As a lifelong learner, I appreciate the team at MasterClass for encouraging learning through renowned experts in their field and giving this opportunity to those most in need via its grants program. Each company has social impact as part of its mission.

During Entertain Impact's sixteen years of doing the work, I have been fortunate to work with phenomenally dedicated and passionate colleagues. The experience and learning from our social impact campaigns make up the book's substance. In particular, Neda Azarfar, our chief marketing officer, provided practical spot-on questions and comments on this book which challenged me and improved the final version. Additionally, Neda's strategy and expertise guided the book's marketing campaign. I also want to acknowledge Holly MacDonald's intersectional perspective in reviewing this material. Helpful contributions over the life span of Entertain Impact came from Allen Bromberger, Andrew Feinberg, Angela Fisher, Daniel Jorge, Elyssa Czynski, Emma Hoffman, Gina Graves, Greg Kapustka, Jesse Highstein, Kristine Moffitt, Marissa Montañez, Mary Croke, Njeri Gachathi, Katie Paine, and Robby Swinnen. Please know that in this book, I write "I" did this, that, and the other, but that's just shorthand for the team at Entertain Impact. There is no I, only we.

Now to those who specifically helped this book become a reality. Firstly, polymath Francis Greenburger gave me encouragement along with guidance on the publishing business and introduced me to Carol Mann, my experienced and caring agent.

My coach, editor, and sounding board extraordinaire, Ellen Daly, guided me through the book proposal and writing process with grace, acumen, and kindness. Then she went the extra mile to recommend the team at Launch My Book. My copyeditor Laura Pitney's probing questions made the book tighter and easier to travel through. Subsequently, Joel Pitney and Jessica Hill handled physical and digital production in a professional no-fuss way. Rochelle Webb's marketing research and initially Paula Amato and then Jane Wesman's PR rounded out the Entertain Impact marketing team.

As I want the reader to read the book and then dip back into it on an ongoing basis, a practical index was vital. The book's index was diligently created by Michelle Guiliano of Line By Line Indexing.

A lawyer who has himself as a client has a fool for a client, so a bow to my literary lawyer Jay Kramer whose wise counsel made my decision making better.

Friends in and out of the literary field have been kind enough to give me their time, experience, and judgment. I'd especially like to give a shout-out to Esther Perel for introducing me to Ellen, my writing coach and to my market researcher. Kudos to Danny Mandil for his insightful feedback on the book proposal; and Michelle Kass and Eddie Sutton for their respective takes on the book publishing world.

To all the other people who supported me while writing *Good Influence*, you have my heartfelt thanks. Each of you are in the DNA of this book.

INTRODUCTION

WE HEARD THE ROAR OF THE one hundred thousand people packed into Philadelphia's John F. Kennedy Stadium long before we glimpsed the scene from our spot backstage. As Billy Ocean stepped on stage, my wife Marie Christine and I clasped hands and looked out over the sea of upturned faces, hardly believing we were there. It was July 13, 1985, and we'd arrived from London just a few weeks earlier. I'd been transferred to New York to help build up the then-fledgling Jive Records and Zomba Music Publishing companies in the United States. Several of our artists, including Billy, were involved with the Live Aid benefit concerts. That's how we found ourselves backstage on that historic day when the music industry came together to raise money for the Ethiopian Famine.

The concert, and a simultaneous one at Wembley Stadium in London, featured over seventy-five artists for the cause. Mega artists such as Queen, George Michael, Elton John, Led Zeppelin, David Bowie, Run-DMC, Madonna, Sade, Santana, the Beach Boys, and Patti LaBelle performed. A worldwide

1

phenomenon in a world with no internet or social media, the concerts were seen on TV by 1,900,000,000 people or nearly forty percent of the world's population. "Do They Know It's Christmas?," the Live Aid single that preceded the show, raised £8 million (twelve times the estimate and over $28 million in 2021 currency). By the end of its run, Live Aid raised over $125 million (over $415 million in 2021 currency) towards African famine relief. The ensuing public pressure resulted in governments supplying grain to end the hunger crisis. For me, this campaign was a massive wake-up call regarding the power of popular culture to create positive change.

Over the next two decades, I followed my passion for music as a senior executive at Jive Records and Zomba Music Publishing. During that time, I had the privilege of working with amazing artists, writers, and producers such as A Tribe Called Quest, DJ Jazzy Jeff & The Fresh Prince (aka Will Smith,), P!nk, Linkin Park, Buddy Guy, Donnie McClurkin, Mutt Lange, Barry Eastmond, Backstreet Boys, NSYNC, Justin Timberlake, and Britney Spears.

In 2003, Jive and Zomba were sold to Bertelsmann, and with some trepidation, I left my Jive/Zomba family for a corporate role at SONY BMG, the Bertelsmann Music Group's joint venture with Sony Music. In the evenings, I attended Teachers College at Columbia University, not for another degree, but to learn more about how education can create positive outcomes for children. During that period, I decided to put together my plan to start an enterprise that would mobilize popular culture, especially celebrities' visibility and reputation, to effect social change.

After two enjoyable years with SONY BMG, I left to start my social impact marketing and advocacy agency, Entertain Impact. I still loved music, and through my company, Eye2Ear Music continued to provide music advisory services to mission-driven music and film organizations. But now, a new passion coexisted: "entertainment for a cause."

Nearly forty years on from Live Aid, I still live in New York City, inspired in part by what I glimpsed that day. I think of myself as a Cultural Change Agent. "What's that?" you ask. My team at Entertain Impact and I create and execute marketing and advocacy campaigns that employ popular culture to raise awareness, support, and funds, inspire action, and drive programs. Over my career, I have done this for numerous philanthropic campaigns and many businesses' campaigns that have a social-good goal.

Entertain Impact is involved in these campaigns in one of two ways. We are either creating and executing the entire marketing or advocacy campaign, or we are adding Influencers into an existing campaign while still having strategic and operational input on that campaign. For the purposes of clarity, I use Influencers as an encompassing term to include social media influencers, public figures, and celebrities collectively. What distinguishes Entertain Impact from other agencies is that we are immersed in the entertainment business and we are exclusively cause-focused on nonprofits, foundations, NGOs, organized movements, philanthropists, and purpose-driven businesses. I have never worked with Influencers for a purely commercial project, and while I have no problem with this, and it would increase revenues, Entertain Impact's mission is to promote causes that have social impact. Fortunately, as the premise of this book shows, social good and financial health are not mutually exclusive.

By engaging Influencers and popular culture, the campaigns Entertain Impact creates or works on shape people's behavior, change policy, and produce systemic change. By so doing, we bring awareness to issues that matter, build coalitions, inspire action, and drive sustainable change. These initiatives move the needle on improving our daily lives and our children's futures.

Some of our most valuable work, though, is the least visible, whether it's advising philanthropists on their foundations, giving pro-bono advice to a just-starting grassroots organization, or facilitating a partnership between an entertainment brand and a major nonprofit.

Our mission is to do the most good for the maximum number of people. We work with international philanthropies developing large-scale public initiatives, community organizations driving local action, socially conscious companies, and individuals exploring ways to give back. Current and past nonprofit and foundation clients include Rotary (polio eradication), The Bill & Melinda Gates Foundation (vaccines), African Wildlife Foundation (wildlife and wildland welfare), and the National Trust's African American Cultural Heritage Action Fund (historic preservation). We also work with purpose-minded businesses such as Participant Media (films), Made in Memphis Entertainment (music), and Time Equities (real estate), and support the philanthropy of well-known celebrities like Kevin Bacon and Usher.

The mobilization of Influencers is key to our successful campaigns. Over the past fifteen years and more than one hundred campaigns, I have worked with over a thousand Influencers, all who donated their time to causes that they felt passionate about supporting. These include actors Lupita Nyong'o, Harrison Ford, and Claire Foy; musicians Celine Dion, John Legend, and Ziggy Marley; business leaders Mark Cuban, Daymond John, and Jeff Skoll; athletes Shaquille O'Neal, Albert Pujols, and John Cena; icons Bill Gates, Queen Noor, and Desmond Tutu; social media influencers Becca Rae-Holloway, Jesmyn Ward, and Jatali Bellanton; and so many more. I have also facilitated social impact marketing campaigns with entertainment properties such as the Oscar-winning Pixar movie *Coco*.

Our clients, though, are the heroes on the front lines—providing urgent health services, protecting our planet, and preventing violence. We're just proud to be part of their team.

What I do, I have named Cause Influence. It is my passion and purpose. I have family and friends who are artists, musicians, sculptors. Their art is a manifestation of who they are, and they are never retiring. Cause Influence is the equivalent for me, and like them, I am in it for life.

How to Use This Book

Many organizations believe they don't have the recognition, connections, or expertise to handle Influencer outreach, so they outsource this function. While this is certainly helpful, in reality, any organization, irrespective of size, can succeed in making an Ask to almost any Influencer on the planet. Most organizations don't, because of a lack of confidence or information. By writing this book, I hope to demystify this process and provide you with the information and tools to engage Influencers yourself.

In this book, I distill everything I've learned into an easy-to-use handbook on creating and executing Influencer-led campaigns. Through practical lessons, stories, and case studies, you have a robust roadmap to guide you, whether or not you have prior experience working with well-known folk. This book shows you how to engage Influencers and, by doing so, reach new audiences. Get your desired audiences to take action, and you'll achieve your business and social impact goals. You can do what I do, irrespective of your organization's size and resources, if you have the confidence and belief that it's possible.

I have divided this book into these sections for ease of reference:

CHAPTER 1, THE INFLUENCER EFFECT, explains the power Influencers exercise and the various models you can use to maximize their effectiveness for your cause or brand campaign.

CHAPTER 2, DESIGN YOUR ACTION PLAN, shows the steps to design and plan your campaign, including how to integrate Influencers to amplify awareness, support, and revenues.

CHAPTER 3, RESEARCH, is an in-depth guide on the best way to find the right Influencers for your campaign.

CHAPTER 4, EDUCATE, gives you the tools and contacts to reach out and cultivate your desired Influencers to promote your campaign.

CHAPTER 5, ACTIVATE, breaks down each facet of your marketing Activations with Influencers to ensure you have the best opportunity for positive outcomes.

CHAPTER 6, MEASURE, provides a practical methodology for measuring the impact of your Influencers and your campaign, interpreting and presenting your findings, and learning from the experience.

CHAPTER 7, MAKE YOUR D.R.E.A.M. A REALITY, sums up the book and proposes a new marketing sector, Cause Influence, that employs the power of Influencers for social impact.

This book's easily digestible information is strategic in thinking and practical to implement. Lessons learned from my successes and failures will reduce your learning curve and promote positive outcomes. I suggest that you read this book from start to finish to have the complete road map. *Good Influence* will also serve as a valuable guide during your campaigns as you encounter specific situations. As needed, dip back into a particular section for support on topics such as writing your Ask letter, measuring your impact, or budgeting for an event.

Several people have expressed concern that I am "giving away the store" by revealing my business practices and trade secrets. My response is, I am happy to do this. The more information I share, the more people do good, and that's a beautiful outcome.

Tools and Resources

In my decades working with celebrities, brands, and non-profits, I've tried many available tools for researching and contacting Influencers, managing Activations, and measuring impact. I've included "Top Tools" throughout the book, recommending a couple of my favorites, both free and paid. The book's companion website, goodinfluencebook.com, contains a wealth of resources, information, and more tools. Check it out regularly for updates and innovations.

Now you can, of course, use the information you learn here to promote your product for purely commercial gain. I come from a business background and have no problem with commerce if done ethically. However, as my agency, Entertain Impact, only works on philanthropic and social justice campaigns, this book will also show how companies, nonprofits and Influencers benefit from cause related work. Further, a central premise of this book is that while businesses, nonprofits, and Influencers can all benefit individually, they and society do far better by working together. Anyone who cares about promoting a cause or enhancing a brand should learn how to engage Influencers for purpose and profit.

Wherever you are in the world, and whether you have a small team or employ thousands, *Good Influence* will help your nonprofit or commercial business grow. If you utilize this information and go about your pursuit professionally, authentically, and persistently, then you'll simultaneously do well by doing good.

CHAPTER 1
THE INFLUENCER EFFECT

*You'll see I influence the world mentally
as well as physically, emotionally, promotionally,
devotionally, socially.*
—RZA, "O DAY"

O N A RAINY SATURDAY MORNING, Devin Howard, a fourteen-year-old New Yorker, is in her bedroom, flicking through Instagram, when she sees Latinx pop superstar Camila Cabello dancing for 23 seconds to Rihanna's "Work" track. Camila's post in support of the American Diabetes Associations' "Diabetes Dance Dare" campaign explains that every 23 seconds, a person in the United States is diagnosed with diabetes. The post ends by daring three musical artists—Shawn Mendes, Diplo, and Ariana Grande—to take up the challenge and dance. Excitedly, Devin runs into her elder brother Jadrien's room and shows him the video. Jadrien is dismissive at first, but when he sees his sporting heroes such as basketball's Shaquille O'Neal and Ishmael Smith dancing in support of the campaign, he gets into the spirit of the challenge.

The siblings rush downstairs and show their mother, Tricia, who recalls seeing a clip of Kelly Clarkson and her daughter doing the "Diabetes Dance Dare" on NBC's *Today Show*. Diabetes is a subject that is close to home since David, Tricia's husband, was recently diagnosed with type 2 diabetes. The entire family does the "Diabetes Dance Dare," challenging family members, and later that day, Dr. Tricia Howard arranges for her staff at the hospital to do the dance and challenge three other medical institutions.

"Diabetes Dance Dare" didn't happen by chance or luck. The campaign was well planned, curated, and executed by my team and me, with input from the then American Diabetes Association's marketing staff. The main goal of raising awareness to prevent or manage the disease was surpassed many times over.

The campaign was nominated for a Shorty Award and generated over 1.5 billion media impressions, including 1.2 billion from original coverage. This success was due to a well-executed creative concept supported by the 70+ Influencers who took part, including Devin Alexander, Kelli Berglund, Garrett Clayton, Mark Cuban, Doug E. Fresh, Diane Guerrero, Kevin Hart, Vicky Jeudy, Usher, and the cast of the NBC hit show Chicago Fire. Traditional media included stories from several national outlets, such as ESPN, the BBC, *The Today Show*, TMZ, Oxygen, *The Huffington Post*, *People*, *Entertainment Weekly*, Billboard, and Redbook. Meanwhile, social media went wild with over 300 million impressions and 12 million engagements in the form of likes, shares, comments, and retweets by over 42 thousand unique authors in the six countries that the campaign organically reached.

The "Diabetes Dance Dare" was a memorable example of what I call "the Influencer Effect" in action.

The Influencer Effect

The "Influencer Effect" is the exponential impact of an Influencer—as defined below—throwing their popularity, social capital, and platform behind a particular cause or brand. The Influencer Effect is both psychological and social, with the intended audience mimicking the actions or recommendations of the Influencer. In my three decades working with celebrities like Usher, Kevin Bacon, Daymond John, Celine Dion, and many more, I've created dozens of such events, large and small, and made it my mission to demystify and break down the Influencer Effect.

The Influencer Effect doesn't always involve an A-list celebrity. An Influencer can be a social media influencer, athlete, local news anchor, author, icon, or even an Instagram animal. In their own way, each serves to shine the spotlight on a worthy cause and thereby channel resources that might otherwise never flow in that direction.

Due to technology—and in particular the smartphone—the speed, scale, and reach of the Influencer Effect is unprecedented in history. When teen pop star Olivia Rodrigo of

"Driver's License" fame met President Biden to promote teen vaccinations for COVID-19, Ana, a teenager in Rio, Brazil, knew about it instantly. Moreover, she had a greater desire to be vaccinated as a result. Whether through word-of-mouth, advertising, or social and traditional media, Influencers, well, influence us all continuously and ubiquitously.

What's more, these Influencers no longer need an intermediary such as a late-night talk show or newspaper article to reach the public. Influencers can directly, immediately, and economically connect you and your campaigns to your desired audiences. Social media allows them to reach and interact with their millions of followers autonomously. Examples are online apologies, PDAs (public displays of affection), and brand or cause promotions.

If you are a business or nonprofit, pay close attention to the Influencer Effect. You can engage a public figure, celebrity, or social media influencer who has a passion for your particular brand or cause, even if you do not personally know them. Maybe it's not the Rock, perhaps it's a lesser-known figure, but that means almost everyone else. In the pages ahead, I'll walk you through my five-step D.R.E.A.M. process for identifying, engaging, and successfully partnering with your perfect Influencer. But first, let's take a closer look at the power of influence and the people who have it.

What Makes an Influencer?

There are several terms used to describe a person who influences us en masse. Three of the most common ones are public figure, celebrity, or social media influencer. I will use "Influencer" to encompass all these and any other related terms for ease of reference. To me, an Influencer is a well-known person who influences desired audiences in a culturally appropriate way for you, your organization, and stakeholders. This term technically can encompass entertainment properties, such as movies and TV shows, which influence us tremendously but are not the focus of this book. This book is concerned with living, breathing Influencers, although an Influencer may, on occasion, have four rather than two feet.

We are all both influencers and influenced. Often our influence only extends to a tiny circle, and we, in turn, are influenced primarily by someone close to us. Your parents probably had the most effect on you, both positive and negative. Many of us cite a schoolteacher who changed our lives. Grammy-nominated artist and hitmaker Bebe Rexha was by her admission a shy, introverted student at Tottenville High School on Staten Island. Bebe credits her music teacher's encouragement to participate in school musicals and join the choir as the impetus to pursue music as a career. Bebe realized she had a strong voice and became more confident. Today, Bebe is an award-winning music artist and Influencer with over 10 million Instagram followers. Many music and other teachers are awe-inspiring and continually change lives.

While the individual influence of a parent or teacher may be crucial to a person's development, this type of influence has a limited scope. The Influencers I am concerned with go way beyond a person's immediate circle and have a ripple effect on a far grander scale. I think of their influence in terms of physics. Namely, the gravitational pull (fame) of a large object (Influencer) creates a force of attraction (for a cause or brand) to other smaller orbiting objects (the public), which alter their course as a result (engagement). In essence, if you trust an Influencer, they will exercise a positive (or negative) influence over you.

In the age of social media, there are thousands of influences—family, friends, workers, media, advertising, and entertainment—pulling at us each day. Each one has the power to persuade someone, subliminally and overtly, to alter their course.

If properly matched, these Influencers get causes and brands onto people's radar screens, and by so doing, give excellent visibility, whether to a particular problem or product. Due to their endorsement, their fans take a leap of faith and follow suit.

Pop sensation Taylor Swift; soccer player Cristiano Ronaldo; spiritual leader the Dalai Lama; make-up artist and performer Jeffree Star; and Jiff Pom, a Pomeranian dog, are all-powerful Influencers with sizable followings and targeted audiences. Cristiano alone has over 300 million followers. Other major Influencers include thought leaders (Seth Godin for marketing, or Esther Perel on relationships), business executives (Paul Polman for the environment, or

Ken Frazer on LGBTQIA+ rights), scientists (Jeff Sachs for the environment, or Neil deGrasse Tyson on science), chefs (Jamie Oliver about health, or Jose Andrés on food insecurity) and civil society leaders (Malala Yousafzai for girls' education, or Bill Gates about health). Occasionally, brands create their own Influencers. Take insurance companies Progressive and Geico, whose spokespersons, Flo and the Gecko respectively, are well-known to the public. Later, I provide advice for how to divide Influencers into manageable categories. For now, know that the Influencer landscape is vast, and you will find the right Influencers for your needs.

A major "A-list" Influencer has a greater ability to attract millions of people towards their fashion choices, eating habits, and of course, social causes. When Angelina Jolie shared with the world her decision to have a double mastectomy due to having the BRCA breast cancer gene, over three-quarters of Americans were aware of the story. Tests for the gene shot up by 64 percent over two weeks and remained 37 percent above the norm six months later.

Influence, put simply, is the ability to persuade a person to do something voluntarily that they were not otherwise contemplating doing. I believe that popular or mass culture, such as music, movies, books, and sports, can do this, and the Influencers who work in these disciplines are change instruments.

Why Engage Influencers?

We all desire to exert influence with the aim, consciously or not, of getting our values, beliefs, and politics accepted by others and persuading them to take action. That action can be buying a product or supporting a cause.

Within my experience, there is one overriding problem that organizations of every size, whether commercial or philanthropic, have in common. Namely, a failure to reach their target audiences and get them to take action.

Combined, millennials and Generation Z (Gen Z) will be the largest US consumer group by 2026 at 30 percent of the population, with spending power of over $1.4 trillion per year. These highly prized groups of young(er) people are distracted by numerous online options, coupled with a very attuned bullshit radar for inauthentic marketing and literally being sold a bill of goods.

Despite spending billions on marketing, corporate America's failure to engage critically needed audiences has led to revenue deterioration, customer erosion, brand weakness, and job losses. The COVID-19 pandemic exacerbated this problem, especially for brick-and-mortar retailers, pushing many companies to the brink of extinction.

Consumer behavior radically changed during the pandemic. Per a McKinsey study, over three-quarters of US consumers began trying new shopping behaviors, and brand loyalty shattered, with Gen Z and high earners the most prone to switching brands.[1] That is why brands use the Influencer Effect—to acquire customers or get them to switch allegiance.

Traditional advertising has little impact on reaching the most coveted generations, but Influencers and their content do. Nielsen's 2015 research shows that Influencer endorsements resonate more strongly with audiences among Gen Z (ages 15-20) and millennials (ages 21-34). Their buying decisions are motivated mainly by social media or celebrity endorsement rather than a brand's advertising[2] or reputation.[3] Nearly 60 percent of Gen Z says they don't mind being pitched by their favorite online social media personality. A study from the University of Arkansas, in collaboration with the Manchester Business School, found that consumers ages 18-24 actively develop their identities and appearance based upon celebrities.[4] They are more susceptible to celebrity brand endorsements than other age groups. For those older folk, an Influencer endorsement still resonates.

The clear and present danger in the nonprofit sector is even more extreme. Hazard a guess at the average age of a US donor. Here's a clue: the answer is in the title of a Beatles song. The average individual donor in the US is sixty-four years old and growing older by the minute.[5] The situation is just as bad in the rest of the world. If younger donors and volunteers don't participate soon, many nonprofits will

1. McKinsey, "Perspectives on Retail."
2. Charm et al., "US Consumer Sentiment and Behaviors."
3. Nielsen, "Global Trust in Advertising."
4. Banister and Cocker, "Cultural Exploration of Consumers' Interactions."
5. Sharpe Group, "12 Interesting Fundraising Statistics."

downsize or cease to exist, depriving millions of the essential services they need to survive.

Large organizations are not exempt. Due to poor planning, research, and execution, many engage Influencers inefficiently and ineffectively. This failure brings about a retreat from what is a clever business play.

Who Should Use the Influencer Effect

Over the last three decades, I have seen the tremendous good and increased commercial benefits resulting from Influencers' involvement in campaigns for nonprofits, for-profit organizations, or both combined. And every day, across the globe, millions of medium and smaller organizations miss out on opportunities to engage Influencers in campaigns to create social change and economic prosperity. The primary culprits for this are an absence of information in the marketplace to demystify the process of engaging Influencers, and a lack of confidence in how organizations like yours could pull it off.

The Influencer Effect benefits:

> **Businesses** with products or services to sell. Influencers will reach your desired audiences more effectively than advertising.

> **Philanthropic organizations, nonprofits, and social justice groups**. An Influencer can help you

inspire people to volunteer, donate, and support your mission.

Politics, faith-based organizations, and interest groups that want to get people elected and legislation or policy passed. An Influencer's endorsement can help persuade voters and your constituents.

Why don't more organizations take advantage of the Influencer Effect? Here are a few rationales I have heard from organizations:

Myth 1: You need to know people
Myth 2: You need big bucks
Myth 3: You need an A-lister to succeed.

None of these are true. Organizations of all sizes have and continue to engage Influencers at no cost, reaching out with a cold call and benefiting from the transformational change that follows. Take Annette Giacomazzi, the owner and creator of CastCoverz, who started her business accidentally. After Annette decorated her daughter's cast, people asked where she bought the decorated cast. Annette began to sell covers for her casts and, with no prior experience, sent celebrities with injuries her cool upbeat covers for their casts. Loris Greiner, Kelly Ripa, and Tamara Monosoff all wore them without any payment or equity participation. The Influencer Effect helped the company rapidly grow to $6 million in revenues. Myriad opportunities exist for you to benefit from the Influencer Effect.

Amplifying Influence Through Multi-Pacts

Substantial academic research and commercial evidence show that brands do even better when engaging in cause-related campaigns. Companies aligning their business and social goals in a focused, direct, and measured manner grow profits, increase shareholder satisfaction, and improve societal well-being.

A corporate partnership I brokered in the early 2000s—between music brand Gibson and my client the Environmental Defense Fund—resulted in a climate-change-themed, limited-edition guitar, which we launched at the Country Music Association Festival. While a powerful tool to bring awareness to the cause, imagine how much more effective this would have been with a maestro like Eddie Van Halen, Eric Clapton, Carlos Santana, Bonnie Raitt, or Buddy Guy playing the guitar and promoting the cause on their tour.

Businesses and nonprofits benefit when each works independently with Influencers. You can, of course, engage Influencers purely for commercial or social purposes. However, when companies, nonprofits, and Influencers combine forces correctly, the positive impact is magnified exponentially. I call this a Multi-Pact, and it unleashes a supernova Influencer Effect best described by the formula:

Business + Nonprofits + Influencers = Amplified commercial & social impact to the Nth degree

While this is happening more frequently than ever before, there are strong business and social imperatives for even more of these collaborations. Industry is spending millions each year on incorporating social impact into every facet of their business. By utilizing the Influencer Effect, these companies save money and achieve their business goals more quickly. One of the most effective Multi-Pacts to date has been "Pour It Forward," which brought together Stella Artois, actor Matt Damon, and the nonprofit he co-founded, Water.org. This Multi-Pact campaign raised approximately $8 million, provided clean drinking water to 3 million people, and enhanced Matt and his organization's reputation. Stella Artois's head of marketing praised the campaign for making the brand "more culturally relevant to young people." He said, "That's been reflected not just in rising sales but in our brand equity as well." Multi-Pacts are a win-win-win.

Most Influencers undertake Multi-Pacts for their own organizations and causes. Yet, there is no reason why more nonprofits and companies that are not owned or founded by Influencers can't work in Multi-Pacts with those or other Influencers. While Multi-Pacts are increasing worldwide by leaps and bounds each year, I encourage more companies, nonprofits, and Influencers to come together in these commercial, philanthropic, and Influencer partnerships.

How the Influencer Effect Benefits You

The Influencer Effect improves your performance, revenues, and social impact. I have seen firsthand how my corporate and philanthropic clients have all gained (im)measurably from employing the Influencer Effect, especially when there is a social-good component. What follows in the sections below are just some of the benefits of the Influencer Effect as demonstrated by research from Nielsen, OC&C, and many other firms.

Audience Connection

Influencers connect your brand or cause directly to new audiences that you may not otherwise reach. They also increase brand awareness with your existing audience. From baby boomers to Gen Alpha, each generation is captivated by and feels a strong connection towards its own set of Influencers. Older generations tend to favor traditional Hollywood celebrities, while younger ones gravitate towards social media influencers. The Influencer Effect is incredibly potent with the highly coveted and difficult to reach millennials and Gen Z. Separate research from agencies Full Screen[6] in 2017 and Takumi[7] in 2020 shows that social media

---

6. Klien, "Trust Digital Influencers."
7. Takumi, "Realities of Influencer Marketing."

influencers on YouTube, Instagram, and lately TikTok, had a greater effect on purchases by younger millennials, Gen Z, and younger, than other forms of advertising by brands. Over 50 percent of the social media generation, irrespective of gender, will consider buying a product if their favorite social media influencer recommends it. Nielsen's 2020 study on an Influencer-led campaign by the Captiv8 platform for a consumer-packaged-goods brand concluded for adults over twenty-five that Influencer involvement meant:

- 90 percent of viewers were aware of the product/brand in the seasoning category,
- 85 percent of viewers would recommend the product to others, and
- 75 percent of viewers would consider purchasing the product.

Business knows the Influencer Effect works. In 2019, an Influencer Marketing Hub survey of executives, including those at brands, marketing, and public relations, found that:

- 92 percent of the people surveyed believed Influencer marketing to be effective;
- 82 percent believed they got a higher quality of customers; and
- 63 percent will increase their Influencer marketing budget in 2020.

Influencer marketing is effective, growing, and here to stay.

Of course, there are sub-segments in each generation attracted to specific Influencers outside of these categories, and your research will uncover these connections.

Raising Awareness

Suppose a cohort of Influencers gets involved in your campaign. If your brand or cause is new, this will help you get noticed, or to stand out from the pack if you're already established. If, say, five Influencers with high numbers of followers each make a post about your brand or cause, you can expect several million people to find out about your campaign. Also, campaigns by brands like the US Polo Association, Red Bull, and Adidas have shown that consumers better recall your brand if an Influencer is involved.[8]

The Bill and Melinda Gates Foundation targeted its 2016 annual letter at young people by asking which two superpowers for good they wished they had. Using the hashtag #superpowerforgood, the Foundation engaged social media influencers to create content, and disseminated it through various online channels. Perhaps the Gates Foundation team had read the study that showed that when an Influencer is part of your campaign, a journalist is 50 percent more likely to cover a philanthropic cause.[9]

---

8. BOOSTO, "Businesses Use Influencer Marketing."
9. Saint, "Celebrity Endorsements Are Still Essential."

In the commercial realm, Pepsi has employed a myriad of music influencers to promote their products for years. Michael Jackson, Shakira, Britney Spears, and the Spice Girls have all drunk a Pepsi for each new generation. These artists each have enormous reach, whether through TV, print, or social media.

Raising Support

A percentage of an Influencer's followers will become active supporters of your campaign.[10] Influencers positively affect consumer attitudes to a brand, give credibility to a product or cause, build brand advocates, and increase consumer loyalty. The hugely successful Ice Bucket Challenge, often emulated but not surpassed, took off at an increased pace when Influencers got involved.

A supporter, whether a customer, donor, or volunteer, is often expensive to acquire through advertising or incentives. There is initial evidence, albeit not unbiased, via a survey by marketing firm Tomoson, that Influencer marketing and emails were the most cost-effective online method of customer acquisition at over double the success rate of advertising or paid search.[11]

10. Allison+ Partners, "Influencers Drive Donations."
11. Tomoson, "Influencer Marketing Study."

Raising Money

Glucose fuels our body, and money fuels business and philanthropy. With money, nonprofits can undertake more social
programs and build out their infrastructure. For nonprofits, one
of the benefits of the Influencer Effect is increased donations. In
2017, worldwide communications and marketing firm Allison+
Partners released an Influence Impact report titled "Powerful
Connections: How Influence, Empathy and Engagement Have
Transformed Cause in the Digital Era" in which they found
that consumers who follow digital influencers (Instagram,
YouTube, and bloggers) are more likely to share information
about and engage with a philanthropic cause. In particular, of
those that follow digital influencers, 35 percent were engaged
with a cause due to an Influencer's recommendation. Of those,
52 percent shared awareness, 51 percent donated, and 37 percent
volunteered. The report demonstrates that Influencers engaged
in cause campaigns drive awareness, donations, and volunteer
engagement at well-above-average rates.[12]

These findings were confirmed by professors Julie Ruth
and Erica Harris of Rutgers, coauthors of "The Relationship of
Celebrity Affiliation to Nonprofit Contributions: A Donations
Demand Model Assessment."[13] Harris and Ruth sampled data
from over 500 charities that had worked with Influencers
across various philanthropic sectors. Findings were that if your

---

12. Allison+ Partners, "New Influence Impact Study."
13. Harris and Ruth, "Value of Celebrity Affiliation," 945-967.

Influencers are athletes, movie stars, or newscasters, you have the best shot at receiving donations. The authors suggest that the public doesn't have the expertise to know if a particular nonprofit is doing a good job. Yet, if they are endorsed by a well-liked—and I would add trusted—Influencer, the public feels the nonprofit has credibility. Credibility equals increased donations and lowers the costs of fundraising campaigns.

This credibility is amplified when an Influencer is affected by the problem the nonprofit is trying to solve. One such example is the late Canadian singer Gord Downie who unfortunately had incurable brain cancer and raised over Can$1 million for research. Why? Because people knew Gord's band, the Tragically Hip, his music touched people, and they wanted to give back.

Again, Multi-Pacts are one of the premier ways of raising money. In 2021, a Multi-Pact formed after I introduced the charity Why Hunger to the producers of CBS TV Special "Play On." Hosted by Kevin Bacon and singer Eve, the show raised $7.3 million for Why Hunger and the NAACP Legal Defense Fund. Why Hunger is now spending the money on not only feeding the hungry but on building movements to address the root causes of hunger and advance the right to nutritious food for all.

Increasing Your Stock Price & Sales

Influencers can have a powerful and unexpected effect on business. According to industry influencer company Tomoson,

every $1 spent on social media influencer marketing gener-
ates a return of $6.50, or a 1:6½ return on investment (ROI).[14]

Traditionally, celebrity—and especially athlete—endorsement of a popular brand will increase sales and stock price.
Influencers get paid tens of millions of dollars to promote
products and services they can genuinely endorse. Think
LeBron James and Naomi Osaka with sports gear, Jennifer
Aniston and Madonna with beverages, and Nicole Kidman
endorsing perfume. Their Influencer Effect is immediate and
palpable. "The Economic Value of Celebrity Endorsements"
by Harvard's Anita Elberse and Barclays Capital's Jeroen
Verleun concluded that an athlete generally has a positive
pay-off in brand-level sales in an absolute sense and relative
to the firm's competitors. An athlete pitching a product also
increased the firm's stock returns. On average, these authors
found that a public company using an Influencer to promote
its brand sees a 0.25 percent increase in stock prices and a 4
percent rise in revenue.[15]

Further, the work concluded that this bump in stock price
sustains and can be boosted by a career triumph. Under
Armour's 2015 stock price went from $64.22 to $104 in a matter
of months when golf endorser Jordan Spieth won the Masters
and US Open that year. Of course, the reverse can be true.
One academic study found that in the three weeks following the revelation of extra-marital affairs by golf superstar
Tiger Woods, three of his most prominent endorsers—Nike,

---

14. Digital Marketing Institute, "Influencer Marketing Statistics."
15. Elberse and Verleun, "Economic Value of Celebrity Endorsements," 149-165.

Gatorade, and Electronic Arts—lost between $5 and $12 billion of their market value.[16] Nike stuck with Tiger, and ten years later, when he won his fifth Masters title in a redemption story par excellence, their stock gained $4 billion, and the brand exposure on TV was worth an estimated $22.5 million.

Adidas must be kicking themselves for not letting Michael Jordan have a signature brand. They passed up the opportunity in 1984, and their fledgling rival Nike, which at that time mostly sponsored tennis and track, embraced the concept, built a new sports line, and earned billions in revenues from Air Jordan basketball shoes. In 2019 alone, Air Jordan had retail sales of $3.1 billion and accounted for 8 percent of Nike's total revenue. This arrangement gave critical momentum to Nike, leaving Adidas behind. Despite engaging Influencers over the years, Adidas never regained their leadership of the sneaker category. Today, Nike reports three times greater revenue than Adidas.

You don't even have to pay an endorser to see the Influencer Effect. Former First Lady and fashionista Michelle Obama's clothing choices during her first year in office, according to the Harvard Business Review, created $2.7 billion in value for twenty-nine companies.[17]

If an Influencer backs up their endorsement with a financial investment in a brand, that commitment can generate even greater gains for all concerned. When Oprah invested in Weight Watchers, the share price increased 92 percent in

---

16. Morain, "Tiger Woods Scandal."
17. Yermack, "Vision Statement."

a matter of days and was up by nearly 300 percent a month later. The Influencer Effect grows your business.

An Influencers' impact on stock price is not always positive, though. When Kylie Jenner, unhappy about social media messaging app Snapchat's redesign, tweeted that she was no longer using Snapchat, the economic results were immediate. Stock of the parent company, Snap, plunged 6 percent, and its market value fell by over $1.3 billion. An Influencer's megaphone is a powerful instrument.

Inspiring Action

The Influencer Effect inspires people to take action by creating urgency to encourage the public to act right then and there. Most often, Influencers will come together around disaster relief, pandemics, or like circumstances to ask the public to behave in a certain way, such as giving money. On September 25, 2021, Elton John performed at the Global Citizen concert in Paris and promoted donations to the WHO Foundation's "Go Give One" campaign that I was working on. Elton asked people to urgently donate $5 to buy one Covid-19 vaccine for someone in one of the many countries that didn't have a stock of these critical vaccines. Better still, donations were being matched up to $1 million by the ELMA Vaccines & Immunization Foundation, and MasterCard hosted the donation site—the manifestation of yet another Multi-Pact. Elton's decades of public prominence, the work of his foundation to combat AIDS, and a concert broadcast to millions all combined to inspire many people to take action. That specific, limited "Go Give One" matching campaign funded hundreds of thousands of vaccines.

The Influencer Effect can also inspire action over a more extended period. I was fortunate enough in 2013 to be involved with Habitat for Humanity's Jimmy and Roselyn Carter Work Project's 30th-anniversary tour. This tour took the former president and First Lady—both well into their 80s—back to New York City to meet the family living in the first house they had helped to build thirty years prior. The Carters have participated in building over 4,300 homes across the globe and across the decades they have inspired hundreds of thousands of people to donate, volunteer, and spread the word through their example. Theirs is also an example of how the Influencer Effect compounds in its impact when other Influencers get involved. The work the Carters were doing inspired many other Influencers to go on work tours with them. Garth Brooks and Trisha Yearwood, for example, connected the Carters to their country music audiences, bringing them on board to the cause. To-date, over 103,000 people alone have gone on builds with the Carters in fourteen countries, and overall, the cumulative benefits to Habitat and its constituents have been immense.

An Influencer's endorsement of a product is powerful social proof and can be compelling if coupled with a CTA. When Kirstie Alley lost over fifty pounds and became diet company Jenny Craig's paid spokeswoman, her messaging that you can do the same propelled the company to new heights of profitability. If an Influencer uses and promotes a product—unpaid—out of genuine interest, this is incredibly persuasive. Here the CTA rationale is be like me by doing like me. Gwyneth Paltrow, Jennifer Lopez, Tracee Ellis Ross, Robert Downey Jr., and countless other Influencers' enthusiasm for the Tracy Anderson Method, an exercise program, and their unpaid promotion through social media, helped build Tracy a thriving business. Tracy's company also integrates social goals into its business goals by providing education on healthy lifestyles for its users, especially teenagers. Combine a CTA with an Influencer and watch the Influencer Effect help you reach your intended cause-focused audiences.

Driving Your Programs

Influencers often loan more than their name to a brand or cause campaign. They are actively engaged. WWE star wrestler and actor John Cena has granted over 650 in-person wishes for sick children for Make-A-Wish Foundation while Angelina Jolie has undertaken more than sixty missions across the globe, visiting refugees and politicians to promote the work of the United Nations Refugee Agency. These Influencers go way beyond helping to raise money and have consistent hands-on involvement with the causes they support.

George Clooney, actor and humanitarian, has worked with Nespresso, a high-end coffee brand, since 2006. First internationally and then in the United States, his involvement has positively shaped the public's perception of the brand and influenced its operations. In 2013, the Swiss company announced that it would develop plantations in Sudan. For many years George advocated to end the atrocities in Sudan, so he was particularly excited to bring together his role as an ambassador for Nespresso with his work to create a better future for the people of South Sudan. Additionally, George has served on Nespresso's sustainability board and has even been critical of Nespresso's sourcing practices in Guatemala. This partnership resulted in 2021's Made With Care campaign, headed by George, that shows that Nespresso cares about and ensures that their supply chain treats their farmers and other stakeholders fairly, sustains communities, and protects the environment.

Changing Culture

New, innovative, and often controversial ideas infiltrate the dominant mainstream culture by moving from the edge to the middle, usually thanks to the arts. Over time the infusion of fresh and vibrant cultural currents cause individuals to alter their behaviors, and then policy and society itself follow suit. Think women's rights, civil rights, and gay rights, all initially shunned but now mainstream. Of course, conservative forces push back against these changing social currents, and so the culture wars ensue. However, time shows who was on the right side of history.

Take the Tony and Pulitzer Prize-winning musical *Rent* which started in an off-Broadway theater in 1996, and over time became a major Broadway musical success, closing in 2008 after 5,123 performances. Its messages delivered in song moved the public to more inclusive and kinder views about the LGBTQIA+ community and those living with AIDS. *Rent* was not the first use of entertainment to break down homophobic barriers. The CBS show *All in the Family* (based on the 1965 UK series *Till Death Us Do Part*), and more recently ABC's 2009 series *Modern Family* and the 2016 movie *Moonlight*, all helped society have a greater acceptance for the LGBTQIA+ community. In a 2008 GLAAD survey, 20 percent of respondents said their views towards gays and lesbians had become more favorable, and over 50 percent of that segment said it was due to the portrayal of gay or lesbian characters in TV and film. By employing the Influencer Effect, GLAAD, the Trevor Project, and other activist organizations have helped mainstream LGBTQIA+ rights. In music alone, Influencers such as Brandi Carlile, Ricky Martin, Miley Cyrus, Lady Gaga, Jessie J, Lil Nax X, and Janelle Monae have helped change culture towards one of LGBTQIA+ acceptance within extensive parts of the younger population.

One of the experts on culture change is Apple, which masterfully employed the Influencer Effect in its 1997's TV advertisement "Think Different." By using 20th-century icons—including Maria Callas, Bob Dylan, Martin Luther King Jr., Pablo Picasso, and Frank Lloyd Wright—Apple invoked the Influencer Effect with incredible results. This advert set a pattern for future Apple campaigns that used Influencers like Karlie Kloss, Paul McCartney, Lin-Manuel Miranda, Serena Williams, Oprah Winfrey, Malala Yousafzai, and Anna Wintour. These Influencers made owning a MacBook—and later an iPhone—"cool," and the Influencer Effect was that millions of people (like me) wanted to join that tribe (even though I logically knew that a PC and Android were probably cheaper and better).

Changing Behavior

Influencers impact how people behave. A special shout-out goes to the fashion industry, whose designers get their customers to change their behavior every year, whether by showing a bra strap, ripping their new jeans, relaxing in sportswear, or wearing sustainable and gender-fluid clothing.

If a favorite Influencer promotes healthy living or our planet's health, people will modify their behavior. Al Gore's documentary *An Inconvenient Truth* changed hearts and minds on global warming. Nearly three-quarters of the public that saw this harrowing warning on the consequences of climate change said they had altered some of their habits.

Anti-smoking campaigns have historically been effective in changing behavior. Recently in China, the World Health Organization engaged four young celebrities—actor Wang Jia, actress Guan Xiaotong, Yiyang Qianxi of the music group TFBoys, and visual artist Chen Man—in a campaign that mirrored the Western ones of prior decades, such as the UK government's "Stoptober," and "Tell the Truth" in the United States. Legacy, an anti-smoking group funded by monies from a $206 billion settlement with the tobacco companies, has even placed shaming ads aimed at celebrity smokers that use the Influencer Effect to get Gen Z to stop smoking. These US-based anti-smoking campaigns have generally been effective in raising awareness and getting people to attempt to quit smoking, but are mostly successful when coupled with support tools.

During the Ebola crisis, the general population in West Africa mistrusted health workers who arrived at their village in protective clothing that made them look like alien invaders from Mars. To combat this, NYU Professor and musician Carlos Chirinos produced several local language versions of the song "Africa Stop Ebola," recorded by Amadou & Mariam (Mali), Taken Jah Fakoly (Ivory Coast), Mory Kante (Guinea), and Didier Awadi (Senegal). The song's lyrics talked about trusting doctors, not touching sick people, and proper sanitation. After hearing the song on the radio, local populations' increased acceptance of medical aid workers saved tens of thousands of lives.

Behavior change can also happen when Influencers highlight a brand's positive traits. Elon Musk's pontifications about the electric car and many other Influencers raising our consciousness about climate change have caused many environmentally-conscious families to invest in a Tesla. They will spend twenty minutes or more at a charging station recharging their Tesla rather than five minutes refueling at a gas station. On the negative tip, childhood obesity is a significant problem in the United States. Pediatric researchers tracked the nutritional quality of food and nonalcoholic brands endorsed by music Influencers and correlated this to their popularity as determined by 2013/2014 Teen Choice Award nominations. No doubt, millions of kids consumed these products because their favorite artists endorsed them. The study's results demonstrated that music Influencers popular among adolescents support energy-dense (read high sugar content), nutrient-poor products. Subsequently, certain researchers have called for strict guidelines on Influencer advertising to children. Influencers and their teams need to be responsible for their endorsement choices since they sway their fans and followers.

Affecting Social Change

Larger companies have utilized celebrities and social media influencers for their social impact campaigns. Lyft was criticized for increasing carbon pollution and traffic congestion despite committing to going carbon neutral. To combat this, in part, Lyft acquired bike-share company Motivate and partnered with basketball superstar LeBron James, professional BMX rider Nigel Sylvester, and twenty-five micro Influencers to offer young people a free year's bike membership. By adding Influencers that align with Lyft's financial, environmental, and social goals, the company improved its brand image with millennials and Gen Z customers, and distinguished the company from rival Uber.

Mid-size and smaller companies can also benefit from a similar Influencer alignment by finding an Influencer who believes in your products or services, or who shares your company's values. Take social media influencer and musician Trill Sammy, a fan of clothing brand Joyrich. After seeing his posts on Instagram, Joyrich gave Trill their clothes. Trill then posted about Joyrich to his nine hundred thousand followers.

The same is true in the nonprofit world. In India, Bollywood actress Anushka Sharma has partnered with the Jaipur Rugs Foundation to support local rural women weavers. By Jaipur Rugs finding global markets for these women's rugs, lives in villages across the sub-continent improved due to the income generated.

Many Influencers have become social entrepreneurs creating social change through their corporate vehicles. Take Newman's Own, a food company that actor Paul Newman started in 1982, where 100 percent of the profits support non-profit causes. Over half-a-billion dollars has been donated to schools and hospitals, veterans, and seriously ill children through Newman's camps. Other examples of Influencer social entrepreneurship abound, such as Jessica Alba's Honest Company and Hugh Jackman's Laughing Man fair trade coffee. I particularly like Studio 189's approach. Cofounded in 2013 by actress Rosario Dawson with best friend Abrima Erwiah, Studio 189 has a store and factory in Ghana. Its clothes are sourced from local artisan communities and are sold at fair prices worldwide. This social enterprise, a part of the United Nations Ethical Fashion Initiative, not only walks the walk but does so in beautiful clothes that inspire us.

Changing Policy

Many Influencers have backed policy changes and gone to federal, state, or city legislatures to support new laws. Take Halle Berry and Jennifer Gardner, who were mad at intrusive paparazzi photographing their children, and did something about it. Their joint testimony before the Californian Senate resulted in a strengthened anti-paparazzi law that protects children of public figures from being photographed or videoed.

Specific political issues can unite strange bedfellows such as Kim Kardashian, Van Jones, and Mark Cuban, who have lobbied for criminal justice reform. On occasions, I have also worked side by side with unlikely allies. In 2019, I cooperated with the leaders of a branch of the Tea Party—the Green Tea Party—on an issue that we both cared about despite having diametrically opposite views in other areas. And, yes, the Green Tea Party is a real thing, and Republicans listen intently to them. I learned that messages to conservatives would be far more effective if they focused on family and faith delivered by an Influencer in a heartfelt manner.

We found common ground in stopping the Trump administration from allowing drilling and ranching on twenty-seven National Monuments. My conservative allies and I believed that these public lands, consisting of millions of acres, were part of our heritage and should be preserved for future generations to enjoy. For the ensuing "Monuments for All" campaign, I reached out to Republican Influencers, including actor Gary Busey, Olympic gold medalist Jamie Anderson, and singer Joy Villa. The campaign consisted of several Influencer appearances at the Conservative Political Action Conference, talk radio, and an op-ed on Fox online.

After a couple of months, the Republican National Committee told the White House that the campaign was hurting the party's midterm election chances and demanded it end. The president stopped implementing his destructive policy, saving twenty-five out of the twenty-seven National Monuments under scrutiny. The incoming Biden Administration rescinded the order and stopped drilling and ranching on the remaining two National Monuments in peril. By finding common ground despite different political views, we helped to achieve a beneficial result for all concerned. If only this model could consistently be adopted on a grander scale, our society would be in a better place.

Further afield in the UK, Manchester United and England soccer star Marcus Rashford grew up poor. His mother, a single parent, worked three jobs to put food on the table and often went hungry to feed her boys. Food insecurity and hunger eradication had always been a cause that Marcus supported. In March 2020, he teamed up with UK charity FareShare to deliver meals to kids who no longer received school meals due to the COVID-19 lockdown. In June 2020, Marcus wrote an open letter to UK Prime Minister Boris Johnson to end child poverty. One day later, the government reversed its policy and agreed to give free school meals for children during the summer holidays. Marcus's letter was a catalyst for change, and his involvement led to over 4 million meals being provided.

Unless the business leader is an Influencer, such as Mark Zuckerberg of Facebook, examples of Influencers testifying before Congress on behalf of a company are rare. I don't know of any. Influencers usually testify on behalf of nonprofits opposing big business such as oil drilling in the Antarctic or requesting more money or action from Congress to fight a social wrong, such as climate change.

The Influencer Effect can also wield soft power by influencing governments through one-on-one meetings, conference attendance, and testifying. Rihanna met with French President Macron in July 2018 when she challenged him on Twitter to do more for education in developing nations. The two then attended the Global Partnership for Education conference in Senegal, where Rihanna spoke and Emmanuel Macron co-hosted. France pledged $248 million toward the cause.

Attracting and Retaining Employees

Businesses today increasingly realize that their customers, shareholders, and employees expect them to be a force for social good. Take millennials, who will make up 75 percent of the workforce by 2025. The 2016 Millennial Employee Engagement Study by Cone Communications revealed that over 75 percent of employees consider a company's social and environmental commitments before deciding where to work. Moreover, a similar percentage would take a pay cut to work for a socially responsible company.

Employee retention and productivity are all heightened when a business practices social good. Successful companies align their triple bottom line—social, environmental, and financial—in a focused, direct, and measured manner. Influencers amplify this and extend these initiatives.

Supporting Political Campaigns

There is a belief that Influencers don't overtly help candidates win elections. A 2019 survey by Hill-Harris found that celebrities didn't persuade 65 percent of respondents to vote for a particular candidate. Yet, if you look below the surface and review the survey across party and age lines, then the story is very different. Specific categories of voters are more likely to vote for a candidate if an Influencer endorses them, particularly those younger, male, non-White, and urban, especially Democrats and independents.[18] Research from the UK backs this up and shows that low political salience respondents, i.e., those who are not focused on politics, are also more likely to seek out information on or vote for a political party endorsed by an Influencer.[19]

A 0.5 percent swing can decide a presidential, congressional, or statewide election. So, if you persuade a statistically significant number to vote for a particular candidate by using the Influencer Effect, you can determine the outcome of an election. For the 2020 Georgia Senate runoff, the Entertain Impact Advocacy Alliance, a 501(c)(4) organization, worked with Black-owned and run D3 Entertainment on a "Get Out the Vote" campaign. Here, five thousand ministers, all local Influencers, were engaged. They, in turn, encouraged their congregants from the pulpit on Sunday and on their social

---

18. Sheffield, "Celebrity Political Endorsements Don't Matter."
19. Veer, Becirovic, and Martin, "Role of Celebrity Endorsements," 436-450.

media platforms to get out and vote. Further support came through placing strategic adverts on gospel radio stations in the days leading up to the election. The Democrats prevailed by a 2 percent margin for the first time in decades, and these Influencers played a part in the unusually high turnout of Black voters.

When Oprah supported then-Senator Obama in his 2008 Presidential election campaign, her Influencer Effect resulted in 1,015,559 additional votes. That accounted for half the popular vote margin in then-President Obama's favor and contributed towards decisive margins in several swing state victories.[20]

Over the years, my agency has utilized the Influencer Effect in the policy area in several ways. In 2007 to promote climate legislation through the Senate for the Environmental Defense Fund, I had a pro-environment major music artist who I had no connection with, and who wished to remain anonymous, write a private letter to the two Californian Democratic senators he knew personally. Simultaneously, I arranged for Jaci Velasquez, a Christian artist, and Dan Boone, the president of the Trevecca Nazarene University, who again I had no connection with, to visit Republican senators to talk about stewardship of the Earth and conservation. The legislation passed the Senate for the first time, but not the House.

Elected public officials crave Influencers. They bask in the Influencers' popularity and hope some of it will rub off on them. This phenomenon is called a halo and is part of the

---

20. Levitt, "One Person, One Vote."

Influencer Effect. One of my most fun political events was the Recording Arts Day on Capitol Hill when I co-chaired the Grammy Advocacy Committee. Here the halls of Congress were invaded by singing musicians, a far better alternative to rioting mobs of right-wing extremists. I recall Linda Sanchez (D–38th district in California) running out of her office to meet Gloria Estefan. Having Gloria as your musical ambassador gave you a far better chance of getting the right meetings or moving an issue forward than if you went solely with ordinary members of the public, like me.

There is no doubt that the right Influencer strategically engaged can profoundly affect election results and the passage of our laws.

Unintended Consequences

There can be positive unintended consequences from the Influencer Effect. One of my favorites is the Activation I undertook for Usher in his hometown of Chattanooga for State Farm's *Neighborhood Sessions* TV series. Each show takes a musical artist back to their hometown to reflect, reminisce, and perform. State Farm produced a concert at Usher's middle school, shot a TV show about him growing up in Chattanooga, and made a sizable donation for philanthropic purposes. This money allowed Usher to fund third-grade arts teachers in over twenty elementary schools, which until then had no art classes. Parents in other grades saw the benefits and also wanted art for their kids. The enlightened school superintendent responded by hiring nine full-time art teachers at the cost of well over $500,000 annually. This is just one example of the many positive unintended consequences I have witnessed from the Influencer Effect. So be ready for a pleasant surprise.

What's In It For the Influencer?

We've looked at the numerous benefits for businesses and nonprofits, but what about for the Influencers themselves? There are several benefits to Influencers using their platforms to persuade us to buy a brand or support a cause. From a purely commercial viewpoint, advertising a brand is profitable for an Influencer. Influencers can get paid millions in hard cash or stock. Rapper 50 Cent got stock instead of a large upfront payment for pitching Vitamin Water. When Coca-Cola bought the company for $4.1 billion, 50 Cent had a $100 million-plus payday.

By associating with a particular brand or cause, an Influencer puts their reputation on the line. So, the one thing they want to know is that the brand or cause is legitimate. There are several cases where Influencers have been embarrassed by being associated with a particular brand or commercial enterprise. Take Hilary Swank, who in 2011 was heavily criticized for appearing at the birthday party of the Chechen leader Ramzan Kadyrov. The authoritarian president had been accused of sanctioning many human rights abuses. Hilary, who denied knowing the situation before her

appearance, apologized and donated her sizable fee to charitable organizations. Around that time, a Turkish company
had approached me to look for high-visibility Influencers for
the same event. After doing my due diligence, I declined to
have any involvement. Management needs to protect their
Influencer clients, and the Influencers themselves have to be
comfortable with, and informed about, each engagement.

I am dismayed when I read about Influencers tripping up
badly due to wrongly associating with a particular organization. This mismatch makes the entire Influencer community
more reticent to engage with philanthropic organizations
that they don't know. However suitable the nonprofit is, the
Influencer may hold back from using their equity and platform
for social good. To help reduce the risk of this happening, I
offer free to Influencers and their teams research, advice, and
program management on their philanthropic engagements
and associations. Detailed analysis usually avoids negative
associations and ensures that the Influencers are involved
with organizations that match their interests and legitimately
do good work.

People often ask if Influencers support a particular cause
to further their career. In my forty-plus years in the industry,
I have not met one who got involved for that reason. All the
Influencers I have worked with do it because they believe in
the cause and want to make a difference. When an Influencer
reveals a challenge, the support they receive and give to others is profound, freeing, and cathartic. Take Demi Lovato,
who bravely came out about her serious mental illness that
had manifested itself in an eating disorder, a heart attack,

and drug abuse. Demi's revelations allowed the public to talk freely about their mental health challenges, and she received substantial support from them in return.

A Growing Field

Influencer marketing is projected to grow to a $15 billion industry in 2022, per *Business Insider*. In 2019 alone, over 240 new agencies and influencer platforms were established. Money flows to Influencers instead of to traditional marketing because the Influencer Effect is direct, intergenerational, and effective.

Today, there are more Influencers and more ways to get content out than ever before. You cannot avoid the Influencer Effect; it is ubiquitous. If done well, the Influencer Effect connects your brands and causes directly to hard-to-reach audiences who pay attention and act. It is one of your top and most cost-effective marketing resources. Making it a strategic imperative is a smart move for every organization, irrespective of size, location, or activities. Business does well by doing good, but can do even better by involving Influencers.

Now that you know the value of the Influencer Effect to your brand or cause, you're ready to learn how to make it happen, not through chance but by following your D.R.E.A.M.

The D.R.E.A.M. Method

Over the last fifteen years of working with Influencers, I have created, developed, tested, implemented, and refined my five-step D.R.E.A.M. method, a combination of science and art to engage Influencers and ignite the Influencer Effect.

Of course, my methodology can be used for purely commercial or political purposes. Still, I hope that people will use the D.R.E.A.M. method to help their fellow humans and our planet by using the Influencer Effect for social change.

These are the five steps to make your D.R.E.A.M. a reality:

> **D**esign your Action Plan
> **R**esearch your Influencers
> **E**ngage your Influencers
> **A**ctivate your campaign
> **M**easure your impact

Both strategic and practical, the D.R.E.A.M. method has resulted in Influencers, businesses, and philanthropic organizations being matched and working together to invoke the Influencer Effect. The outcomes to date have been impressive, and you can benefit similarly in the future.

CHAPTER 2
STEP 1: DESIGN YOUR ACTION PLAN

No alarms and no surprises, please
—RADIOHEAD, "NO SURPRISES"

A S THE VENERABLE CHINESE philosopher Lao Tsu stated, "A journey of a thousand miles begins with a single step." Maybe so, but you still need a GPS to find your way. Creating an Action Plan is essential. It functions as your campaign's GPS, mapping every facet of your journey in detail.

Creating an Action Plan ensures you understand what you are getting into, the resources you need, who will do what tasks, the timelines involved, and the anticipated results. I have often seen organizations with an upcoming anniversary or event fail to allow enough runway to create and execute its Action Plan. Some don't even have an Action Plan at all.

From an Influencer integration perspective, there are two ways to approach any Action Plan. You are either creating the campaign from scratch or integrating Influencers into an existing one. It is much easier, cheaper, and quicker to incorporate Influencers into a pre-existing campaign than to create the whole campaign. So, if you already have your campaign's Action Plan and simply need to integrate Influencers into it, then you could go directly to Step 2: Research. However, I'd recommend you still read through this chapter to ensure that your existing Action Plan covers Influencer integration comprehensively. For those of you who need an Action Plan, I will show you how to create a campaign from the ground up that incorporates Influencers and manifests the Influencer Effect.

Are You Ready for Action?

First Do a Needs Assessment

When advising an organization that wants to engage Influencers, I first do a needs assessment. This simple scan can determine whether your organization is ready to engage Influencers. Say for example that your board is uncomfortable having an Influencer represent your organization. Better to nix the idea until you can persuade them of the benefits. You'll find plenty of ways to do just that in this book.

To undertake a needs assessment, create a simple scorecard with the categories you feel essential. I use:

- board buy-in
- budget
- cultural fit
- donor or customer identification
- email and social media program effectiveness
- staff commitment
- website engagement

Give each category a score from one to five. Then if the score in each category is three or above, you are probably in good shape to move forward. For those areas where the score was less than three, you'll probably need to do some remedial work.

The vast majority of organizations I encounter are ready to work with Influencers. If they aren't, I show them how to remedy the deficiencies identified in the needs assessment and quickly get to the starting line.

Get Your Ducks in a Row

There are several ducks, if not all, to get in a row before you start to build your Action Plan.

Build Your Team

Build your Action Plan alone or with a small team. Too many Action Plans get stuck in committee and never emerge. Factor in your team's strengths and weaknesses. I am good at strategic thinking and networking. But if God is in the details, I must be an atheist. Fortunately, my team is strong at planning, execution, and tracking. Together we do the whole job. And in case you didn't read the acknowledgments, I'd reiterate what I said there. In this book, I write "I" did this, that, and the other, but that's just shorthand for the collective team at Entertain Impact and their work. I would suggest that, like us, for each campaign, you designate one person to deal with your Influencer relations.

To get information and buy-in, be curious and ask questions from a wide array of internal and external sources. I find that friends, aligned organizations, or even competitors are a good source of knowledge and perspective. Many have relevant white papers, blogs, and interviews on their websites and social media relating to Influencers, how they have engaged them, and the results. Several academic services such as Academia and Statistica provide articles and research on various pertinent Influencer areas at little or no cost. Just make sure your sources are reputable, valid, and complete.

Get Outside Help

Engaging Influencers requires specific skill sets. Consider whether you need to hire external support such as a talent-relations or public relations (PR) firm to cover those areas where you have knowledge gaps. I have used consultants or freelancers for creative content, measurement, and on rare occasions, talent outreach. They have the expertise or connections needed for a particular campaign but are not required full-time. If you need outside help, the best way is to get a referral. Failing that, experts are a click away. Go to freelancer aggregator websites such as Fiverr or Upwork. You set your terms and prices, and people apply. Each applicant has helpful rankings and reviews. I've had good experiences with this approach.

Identify Free Services

Most midsize and larger organizations create Action Plans using their internal team, or they hire me or someone like me. Smaller ones, by necessity, do the job themselves. But if you are a nonprofit of any size, remember the phrase "pro bono," Latin for free professional services. Many firms, including legal, marketing, and PR agencies, will work without charge or at drastically reduced rates for philanthropic causes. Consumer brands often make pro bono contributions by donating products that support a campaign which simultaneously promotes their brand. This conscious capitalism doesn't only benefit the recipient but also the provider. Having an Influencer's name or the promise of Influencer involvement attached to your campaign will improve your chances of success.

One aspect of pro bono that I like is a charrette, or round table, of third-party experts not connected with my client who voluntarily give three hours of their time, wisdom, and brainpower to ponder an important question. My first experience of this was when I was one of those experts at a charrette for the then-Brady Campaign to Prevent Gun Violence. A professor, lawyer, chief marketing officer, social media expert, and I spent an afternoon brainstorming how to overcome the most significant objection Brady's opponents used to block the campaign's goals: gun control curtails people's freedom to carry guns under the second amendment. Out of that charrette came the campaign "We Are Better Than This," which avoided the second amendment, proposing that we are better than a nation where guns murder thirty-two people every day. Entertain Impact then worked on creating PSAs. The parents of students killed, the survivors of various mass shootings, police officers against gun violence, and Influencers like Mark Ruffalo, who suffered a family tragedy through gun violence, all made appearances. The Influencer Effect kicked in, people took note, and Brady had one of their most successful campaigns ever.

I use charrettes sparingly since people are busy, but they have other beneficial outcomes. Many of the participants will volunteer for your organization. For example, after a charrette for Kevin Bacon's philanthropic organization SixDegrees.org, Chase Bank's head of nonprofit technology donated hundreds of hours of tech time and included SixDegrees.org in a hackathon contest for college students. Charrettes usually require work to organize, but each one I have done has proven more than worthwhile.

Choose When to Start

It takes time to D.R.E.A.M. If you integrate Influencers into your campaign, allow as long as possible before the campaign launch. The ideal is six to nine months if you are creating your campaign from scratch, and if the campaign already exists, then the minimum is three to six months. When I have had less time to engage Influencers, outcomes were less successful. So now, I pass on a project if the deadlines are too tight.

Set Your Timetable

Time is the one commodity we can never replace. Yet certain organizations seem to feel it's an elastic concept and have endless meetings and long turnaround times for providing information or creating work product. I would highly recommend completing your Action Plan within a maximum of twelve weeks. Mine would look like this:

Action Plan Timeline

Kick-off meeting—week one
Gathering information—weeks two through four
First draft—weeks five through six
Feedback—weeks seven through eight
Final draft—week nine
Buy-in and green light—week ten
Contingency—two weeks

Irrespective of the size of your organization, no later than three months from kick-off, you should have a complete, functional, and ready-to-implement Action Plan.

Now Create Your Action Plan

My philosophy when creating campaigns has always been to wrap serious subjects up in entertaining packages. I find this approach attracts people to your brand and cause. Facts are needed, but enjoyment garners audiences and makes your campaign memorable.

Now that you have put your building blocks in place, you can move forward and create your Action Plan.

Action Plan Step 1
Campaign Goals

Set an intention. Does your campaign wish to create awareness, attract support, inspire action, grow market share, or increase revenues? Whatever the reason, make these goals fit with your mission.

Ask yourself, "What would my campaign's champagne moment be?" You may not necessarily adopt the answer as your goal, but you can find out much with this question. Project to the end of your campaign as if you had achieved this big win. What would have changed? Your answer here can be very enlightening.

Like the Russian matryoshka dolls, there are goals within goals. Don't be satisfied with your first answer. Drill down further. This approach will reveal what goals you adopt. Often the goal will appear straightforward, such as increasing the number of email subscribers. However, implicit in this answer may be another goal, such as to increase donations from those email subscribers. Even within this goal hides another: to raise money so that more health workers can be trained in West Africa. However, training health workers is well beyond the control of your campaign, so be selective in identifying and choosing those goals that your campaign can be directly responsible for achieving. The good news is that, as you will learn in detail in chapter 6, your goals are measurable.

I prefer to set up three to five S.M.A.R.T. goals for a single campaign. S.M.A.R.T. goals are Specific, Measurable, Achievable, Relevant, and Time-bound. The more precise your goals, the more achievable they become. Influencer-specific goals tend to fall into three main categories.

Top-Line Campaign Goals

Identifying Influencer involvement as part of your top-line campaign goal needs to be very specific. Vague goals, such as raising money for cancer, lead to disappointing results. Better stated and more likely to happen is, "To raise $1 million in eight weeks through a Multi-Pact campaign between Genentech, Stand Up To Cancer, and Influencers such as Morgan Freeman, with a television, online, and retail component."

Influencer Characteristics and Engagement Goals

Spell out the exact number and type of Influencers you want
to engage for your campaign, and specifically how you
want them to engage. "I want two Influencers for my
campaign" is an amorphous goal, and needs specificity.
For example, you might write, "The upcoming campaign goal is to get two Influencers at an Ambassador
level who promote leadership, land sustainability, and
economic empowerment, and who appeal to donors in
the USA, and for those Influencers to undertake a trip
to East Africa, meet with heads of state, and appear in a
marketing campaign activation including social media
posts, events, and media appearances during the initial
three months of the campaign launch."

Influencer Commitment Goals

Identifying your goals for the Influencer's commitment—
whether for the duration of the campaign or longer-term—
is essential. "Establishing a long-term relationship with an
Influencer" is an aspirational goal. However, commitment
goals need to be precise. For example, you might decide
that your goal is "to secure an Influencer who (a) appeals
to the majority of our campaign's desired audiences,
(b) will be a spokesperson for us, and our work for the
12 months following the start of the campaign; and (c)

agrees to undertake no less than three specific marketing Activations within that period, such as social posts, attendance at an organizational event, and field visit."

Action Plan Step 2
Who? Defining Your Audience

Defining and knowing your audience is one of the most crucial parts of any Action Plan. If you don't know the audience you are trying to reach, how can you find effective Influencers to get to them, no matter your resources? Ten years ago, I worked on the Bill and Melinda Gates Foundation's "Art of Saving A Life" campaign, which engaged over thirty artists to produce art in the cause of global vaccines. A former staffer at the Gates Foundation defined their target audience as any member of the general public who would take action. This description is too vague for me.

Knowing your audience in detail means you know which Influencers are best to reach them efficiently and at the lowest cost. For the nonprofit Promundo and the Kering Foundation's "Global Boyhood Initiative," you may have thought young social media influencers would have been appropriate. However, our research showed that Kevin Bacon was a strong match for their desired audience segment: parents. I created a four-minute Instagram TV interview with Kevin on raising boys, which boosted the campaign's reach and impressions over a hundred-fold.

For the IFC cable company's movie *The Man Who Knew Infinity* about the gifted mathematician Ramanujan, the campaign focused on STEM organizations, academics and students, and the Indo-American community. This targeted approach, honing in on a defined audience segment, led to outreach to over 120 diverse math organizations across the United States with over 3 million members, an Obama White House panel on science, and the launch of a worldwide math competition, "The Spirit of Ramanujan." While the leading Influencers were the movie itself, along with the actors Dev Patel and Jeremy Irons, I also added two math- and science-based Influencers— Field Medal Winner (the Noble Prize for Mathematics) Manjul Bhargava, and mathematician and businessman Stephen Wolfram. The Influencer Effect resulted in twice the average trailer view rate and one of IFC's highest box office grosses.

A 2005 Harvard Business Review article "Marketing Malpractice: The Cause and the Cure" by Christianson et al. suggested in part that a lack of audience segmentation causes 90 percent of product launches to fail.[21] Audience segments are subgroups of your target audience. I have worked on campaigns initially aimed at voters, college kids, and soccer moms. Each of these was too broad for my liking, and we broke those broad categories down. In the United States, to define your audience as Latinx is amorphous. Over 60 million people, or 18 percent of the US population, are of Latin origin. It's far easier to picture reaching out to "a mother with two kids under the age of seven of Mexican heritage with a

---

21. Christensen, Cook, and Hall, "Marketing Malpractice."

master's degree living in a suburb of LA with a household income of over $100,000" than a generic Latinx woman. The better you define your audience, the better your chance of finding the right Influencers to reach them.

By breaking your target audience down into specific audience segments, you will be able to precisely identify the people you want to reach, which Influencers are appropriate, and the best ways to do so. Take Paul Trible and Paul Watson, founders of the shirt business Ledbury. They knew that business executives were their number one target audience and sent samples directly to MSNBC's on-air personalities Joe Scarborough and Willie Geist of *Morning Joe*. Their instincts were right on: Geist liked the shirts, became a customer, and gave Ledbury an on-air shout-out. The brand's founders went on to be featured on MSNBC's show *Your Business*. They tapped into a large niche market segment by not trying to be all things to all people. The Influencer Effect caused a 20 percent growth in their business.

If you don't know your audience, you increase the chances of making a mistake with your marketing approach. The Co-op, a supermarket chain in the UK, ran a local print ad campaign that suggested parents reward their daughters with a chocolate Easter egg for "doing the washing up." This campaign did not occur in 1817 but rather two centuries later, in 2017, when social norms were far different. After an anti-sexist backlash storm on social and national media, the Co-op, which comparatively had a positive record on gender, apologized. Unfortunately, the brand damage was done, and the chain was seen as old-fashioned and outdated.

Below are some suggestions for how to think about creating audience segments for your campaign.

Public Audiences

Within the public audience, there exist many characteristics that can be used to categorize and define your target audience. Below you'll find the ones I use. Being clear about this information will help you find Influencers who reflect these traits and connect your campaign to your audience.

Demographics and Psychographics

Using demographics and psychographics, you can more precisely dissect your targeted audience, resulting in significantly higher odds of Influencers connecting directly to each segment.

Demographics look at people or sub-populations' external characteristics, such as age, race, and sexual orientation. These, though, are the basics. Each group has many variants and nuances. Look at their social and economic data, birth, marriage, and death rates, family structure, education, average income, occupation, religion, and geographical location are all factors to break down your audience.

If you delve deeper into their psychographics, you will know your target audience even better. Psychographics deal with the internality or mentality of sub-populations, including attitudes, opinions, and interests. These, in turn, can be broken down further to include factors such as personality, values, beliefs, and lifestyles.

You will have enough categories to create audience segments between demographics and psychographics. The "how" to reach them comes later in your Action Plan. The deeper you drill down and identify the data points for each group you wish to reach, the more likely you will match the right Influencer.

Generational characteristics

An excellent place to start breaking down your audience is by generation. In the West, there are five generations. They are:

- The Silent Generation (1900-1945)
- Baby Boomers (1946-1964)
- Generation X (1965-1980)
- Millennials (1981-1996)
- Generation Z (1997-2012)
- Generation Alpha (2013 to 2028)

Plenty of resources exist where you can find a breakdown of the generational personalities and preferences, musical likes, buying habits, and much more. While these charts are helpful, they are only a starting place.

Take Gen Z, a desired demographic for brands and cause campaigns alike. There are approximately two billion members of Gen Z—or 30 percent of the world's population. Seventy-one million Gen Zers reside in the United States alone, so to say this is a homogenous group, that they all like the same music or food, will not help you. However, there are a few trends that can be helpful. Gen Z grew up with technology, so their communication style is text-, IM-, and social media-heavy. Contrast this with the baby boomer generation, which prefers face-to-face meetings or telephone calls. Motivational factors between these generations also vary. Gen Z's work ethos is creativity, diversity, and individuality, while boomers are motivated by loyalty, teamwork, and a sense of duty.

Geography

National, regional, or local audience insights are significant. Don't take a bland or generalized approach; see the colors, the distinctions, and variations, then factor these into your process for Influencer connectivity.

A person who lives in Los Angeles and a person who lives in Memphis—both cities I know well—are nearly as different as their counterparts in Stockholm and Milan. Sure, the latter speak different languages, but don't be fooled by a common language in the United States. Language hides significant cultural, political, and economic differences.

Within one region, there can be pronounced differences between audiences. A person who hails from rural Georgia has different values than their urban counterparts.

Even within one city—such as my home, New York—areas like Staten Island are far more conservative and homogeneous than others, like Queens, which is the most diverse county in the United States, with over 100 countries represented. You'll need to engage different Influencers for different audience segments.

> **PRO TIP:** *Don't try to be all things to all people. You may have identified ten audience segments, but you best apply the 80/20 rule and focus on getting Influencers and allocating resources to the top categories that make up most of the people you wish to target.*

Listen

Audiences are living breathing people, not statistics. Rather than impose your views upon them, listen to what they want. Millennials' and Gen Z's desire to incorporate social purpose into their careers and life choices is crucial in reaching them via Influencers.

> **PRO-TIP:** *While each audience segment is unique, acknowledging our interconnectedness and interdependency is a mindset that will serve you well.*

Top Tools

Various tools such as Strategyzer's Value Proposition Canvas will help you look at the pains and gains of your target audiences and see how what you provide will help them. Use this free template, and you will put yourself in your audience's shoes and feel more attuned to their wishes. This tool is equally helpful to put yourself in the Influencer's shoes.

Business Audiences

Influencers

Once you have identified your public audience segments, set out in the Action Plan the characteristics, number, location, and other pertinent factors you'd like your Influencers to have. This process will help you hone in on the archetype Influencer that is the right fit when you start full-blown Influencer research for your campaign. I'd also sprinkle in a few possible Influencer names into your Action Plan, as this makes the plan real and excites readers. Just add a disclaimer that the names are for illustration purposes only.

Pro Tip: *If you have less than the optimal time to get Influencers involved with your campaign, here's a suggestion. Once you have identified your audience segments, you can, in tandem with finishing your Action Plan, start Step 2: Research. This workaround will save you several weeks.*

Partnerships

Partnering up with other entities can raise your profile, reach, and revenues. A partnership is a mutually beneficial relationship with each entity taking on the risk and benefiting from the promotional returns. These can be as simple as joining your local grocery chain's rounding-up program or as complex as partnering with a powerhouse movie to promote your cause. The partner should complement your brand, and vice versa. Take GoPro and Red Bull. Neither are in the same product category but are both energetic lifestyle brands. They came together for a literal out-of-this-world collaboration: a free-fall jump by Influencer Felix Baumgartner from a space pod more than twenty-four miles above Earth's surface.

Media partnerships in particular can significantly advance your brand or cause. One such opportunity for the ELMA Music Foundation's Music & Youth Development Alliance came from Kevin Bacon. CBS *Good Morning* was doing a segment on Kevin to promote the Showtime show *City on the Hill*. Kevin had CBS shoot him and his co-star Aldis Hodge as they toured a youth community center in New York called The Door. Utilizing the arts to engage young LGBTQIA+ adults, The Door then provides wrap-around services such as health, legal advice, education, and job training. The segment's airing increased awareness and interest in The Door from the public and donors.

One of the most successful cause-related Multi-Pacts was a partnership between cable channels, the American

Society for the Protection of Cruelty to Animals, and singer Sarah McLachlan. Sarah licensed her track "Angel" and appeared in the public service announcement (PSA), and specific cable channels agreed to give airtime to run this powerful appeal at no upfront cost in return for a share of the revenue raised. Sarah, an ardent animal welfare advocate, saw her song contribute not only to raising ASPCA's profile but also to significantly expanding its programs. The public responded by donating over $30 million via 200,000 new donors, many of whom became monthly givers. While each partner gained from the collaboration, the biggest beneficiaries were the animals needing ASPCA protection.

Sponsorships

Sponsorships are different from partnerships—although the terms are sometimes used interchangeably. Sponsors will pay money or donate goods or services in return for an association with your campaign or event that promotes their brand. The biggest sponsorship deals are for major worldwide events such as the 2020 Summer Olympics. Here, Airbnb, Alibaba, Coca-Cola, and other major corporate brands collectively paid billions of dollars for the association with the Olympics, and then millions more to the Influencers that represented their brands. Coca-Cola's six-pack of four Olympic champions, one Paralympic champion, and one hopeful champion, is an example. On a smaller scale, how often have you been to a music show and seen advertising promotions for a bank or telecom company on the screens, or in the marketing materials? Touring musical acts, big and small, offer opportunities to promote your brand or cause. Philanthropically-minded artists will partner up to promote a cause at their concerts, whether teen suicide prevention, addiction treatment, or hunger relief. These artists and other Influencers' commercial endeavors are gateways to audience segments corporate America wants to reach.

> **Pro Tip:** *If you are a nonprofit, whatever your size, having an Influencer involved makes it more likely you will get a sponsor involved.*

Multi-Pacts

If you enter into a Multi-Pact—the optimal choice for many cause campaigns—you'll need to identify your co-campaigner, whether a nonprofit or business. Choosing the right partner makes life easier and improves outcomes.

Nonprofits

Suppose you are a company or brand that wishes to seek out a nonprofit partner. We have seen that Influencers need to be an appropriate cultural fit with your organization, and this rule applies equally to your nonprofit partner. Nonprofits need to align not only with your social goals but also with your business and environmental ones. Take dairy producer Dannon, who teamed up with nonprofit micro-lender Grameen. Together, they built a yogurt factory in Bangladesh that created jobs and produced low-cost yogurt with added nutrients that fight disease and malnutrition. Grameen's contribution was to permit anyone to sell the yogurt, providing micro-loans as start-up capital. The Influencer promoting the cause campaign was Grameen's founder and Noble Peace Prize Laureate Muhammad Yunus, a national hero in Bangladesh and a big deal in many circles worldwide. This Multi-Pact produced massive benefits: healthier kids, jobs at the factory, and a livelihood for women sellers in the villages. Dannon benefited not only from the social impact; they benefited financially from taking on a new venture and introducing a new product line. Muhammad Yunus fulfilled Grameen's social mission and several personal goals. This was again a win-win-win.

To find out more about a nonprofit, undertake research just as you would for an Influencer. Ask searching questions. Are the senior team and board respected? Have there been any scandals? Are they effective in their mission? Here are a couple of specialized searches to undertake:

• Charity Navigator: rates nonprofits based primarily on what percentage of every dollar raised goes to programs. To get the top four-star rating, the nonprofit must direct 92 cents or more of every dollar to programs. While helpful, I've always felt the ratings were one-dimensional, and instead Charity Navigator should rate how effectively each nonprofit is in fulfilling its mission. Suppose only forty cents of every dollar goes to programs; yet, the nonprofit's impact is higher than more fiscally conservative organizations. Isn't that better? Fortunately, Charity Navigator introduced in mid-2020 its Encompass Rating System to rate smaller, newer, and some larger nonprofits that didn't previously qualify under the star rating system. The four criteria are finance and accountability, impact and results, leadership and adaptability, and culture and community. This new system has increased the number of nonprofits rated from 9,000 to 160,000 and is a step in the right direction.

- Tax Form 990: Every nonprofit in the United States must make its federal tax filing, the IRS Form 990, available to the public. This form shows a nonprofit's income sources, expenses, amounts over $100,000 paid to independent contractors, grants made, and the board and senior staff's compensation. Combine this with an annual report, and you'll know a lot about your nonprofit partner and how it spends its money.

PRO TIP: *Restricting donations to nonprofits for programmatic use only is counterproductive. Nonprofits need qualified staff, technology, and all the other items that business needs to be effective.*

If you are a nonprofit looking to partner with a company or brand, make sure that you have an authentic connection with them. Do your due diligence to ensure that the brand is reputable, just as you would when checking if an Influencer is right for you.

On rare occasions, a company will attach a nonprofit partner to a campaign to brandish its image while not fully believing in the nonprofit's mission. Take greenwashing, for example, where companies falsely market themselves or their products as environmentally friendly when they are not. In the past, Exxon Mobil promoted its reduction of greenhouse gas emissions when the reality was an increase. If you were an environmental organization that took money from Exxon Mobil, your credibility would be severely damaged.

When you find like-minded and authentic businesses to partner with, see if they engage Influencers for commercial purposes. If they do, co-opt them to your cause-related campaign by forming a Multi-Pact. The gold star over the last decade-plus has been the "One Pack = One Vaccine" partnership between Proctor & Gamble's Pampers brand and UNICEF. For every specially marked packet bought, Pampers donates the cost of a vaccine to fight maternal and newborn tetanus. Various Influencers, from appropriately named Baby Spice Girl Emma Burton to UNICEF spokesperson Salma Hayek, have raised the profile of the campaign. By 2019 the campaign had vaccinated and protected 100 million women and babies worldwide, contributing to saving over 500,000 babies' lives and eliminating maternal/neonatal tetanus in twenty countries. This Multi-Pact was a perfect combination of UNICEF, Pampers baby products, and Influencers who were also mothers.

> **Pro Tip:** *When an Influencer or their team is determining whether to engage with a nonprofit or business, it is best for them to use the same criteria in vetting the opportunity before signing on, e.g., determining whether there an authentic fit and assessing the professionalism of the organization.*

Action Plan Step 3
Developing Your Campaign Creative

Create Clear Messaging

Clear messaging allows you to connect to your audiences in a way that they understand and that compel them to take action. Don't assume that your audience will know you or spend the time to do research to get to know you. Your messaging needs to ask for what you want directly. The "Diabetes Dance Dare" was a massive success in raising awareness but didn't raise a comparable level of donations. Unfortunately, the reason was simple, and against my recommendation: the messaging did not include asking for money. Guess what? Awareness went through the roof, but the money raised wouldn't have paid to repair the hole.

As this relates to Influencers, there are specific considerations which will help hone and improve the way you communicate.

Pre-launch

Influencers are not only your messengers but also the first litmus test of whether your messaging resonates. If your messaging is not strong when you reach out to get Influencers on board, it will be a turnoff and reduce your chances of success. Influencers want to promote messaging that they are comfortable with and believe effective. Remember that many Influencers' tools are words, so they are a discerning audience. Listen to Influencer feedback.

Adaptation

When you send messaging—including the hashtag—don't be surprised if your Influencers adapt it to their voice, and you only find out when they post or speak to your audience. For the National Trust's African American Cultural Heritage Action Fund's campaign to preserve Nina Simone's childhood home, the hashtag used was #savingplaces, and most Influencers such as John Legend and Cat Stevens used this. Fortunately, the rapper Noname adapted it to #SaveNinaCrib, which went viral and got significant media pickup. An Influencer reworking your message is good because they infuse the message with their persona and authenticity.

Different Influencers, different messages

Your campaign messaging will have an overarching theme but may need to be adapted for each audience segment, and various Influencers will deliver it differently. For the campaign to prevent mining, ranching, and farming on vast swaths of public land known as National Monuments, my client and I created different but related messaging for two diametrically opposite audiences. For conservative conservationists, the focus was on family, faith, and American patriotism, while the messaging that resonated with progressive environmentalists related to pollution, big business, and preventing the elimination of small stakeholders. The common theme for both groups was the need to preserve the land for our children and generations to come. Influencers from opposite ends of the political spectrum delivered these different but related messages for each audience. As a result of many groups' collective efforts, not just our campaign, former President Trump rescinded his executive order to allow commercial activity on National Monuments, and millions of acres were saved from imminent destruction.

Choose Your Call to Action

With any campaign, you want to ask your audience to take action, and by not doing so, you are missing a huge opportunity. Your ask is known as a call to action, or CTA. Some of the most common CTAs are learn, share, volunteer, buy, and donate. Popular CTAs for nonprofits are signing the pledge, contacting your representative, and joining a fundraising team. Top CTAs for businesses are shop, subscribe, review, and recommend. To my mind, liking a social media post is not a compelling CTA, so carefully consider how your CTA ties back to your campaign goals.

A vague CTA is unhelpful and self-defeating. However good your Influencer is, if you don't ask for a clear action, or confuse your audience with opaque messaging, you will get zero response. Being direct and succinct with your CTA yields audience engagement. Contrast these examples:

1. We can end hunger if we work together
2. $2 = one meal
3. Donate—$2 buys one child a meal

To me in a time when we are busier than ever and bombarded by so many requests for our time, a simple message like the third one above works best.

My experience is that once the public is made aware of a problem or challenge, they will react positively, compassionately, and generously. Equip your Influencers with compelling messaging, connect to your audience, and watch the Influencer Effect do the rest.

Create Cool Content

Your content, especially visual content, is one of the best ways to connect your message to your target audience and entice them to want to learn more. You do this by creating cool content combined with compelling messaging, asking them to take action, and directing them to a place where they can do so.

Most organizations want to tell their whole story in one video or blog that takes forever to read. Given that Gen Z's attention span is on average eight seconds, and millennials only four seconds longer, the Influencer's content better be short and sweet. I recommend videos under one minute, and for social media, under fifteen seconds is optimal. Each piece of content should make one central point and have a CTA. Whether your Influencers appear in the content or simply post it, they will ensure that each video has a shot of being seen by your intended audience.

Even for long-form content, keep it short. For Promundo and Kering Foundation's "Global Boyhood Initiative," I executive produced an IGTV interview series with Influencers Kevin Bacon, Ziggy Marley, Justin Michael Williams, and Chelsea Hill. Each five-minute episode was inexpensively shot via Zoom and mostly by iPhone.

Over the years, I have produced and adapted content with Influencers inexpensively and with tight timelines by adapting existing materials. For Rotary's "End Polio Now" campaign, I took an existing music video, "Personal Revolution" by Ziggy Marley, and intercut archival footage celebrating polio health workers from our client Rotary. I am always amazed by the generosity of the Influencers I work with who never charge for their services and provide materials such as videos at no charge.

When it comes to content creation, use creative people, not those that make generic, dull, and tired material that is not distinguishable from anyone else's work. Ask for recommendations, watch not just the highlight or showreel but your candidate's full-length productions. This due diligence will save you time, money, and stress down the line. An Influencer's day job is to appear in professional productions that are to a high creative standard. If you produce content of this high quality, you will increase the number of Influencers who will sign up for your campaign.

Be Sensitive to Cultural Adaptation

The most apparent cultural adaptation to watch out for is whether your campaign needs to be produced in a language other than (or in addition to) English. A significant portion of the population speaks Spanish in the United States, so this needs to be considered should you be targeting this demographic. In comparison, worldwide organization Rotary translates all its materials into six languages.

An Influencer's language and accent can be a factor when choosing who to work with. International medical organization ALIMA's "#WeAretheSolution" campaign was focused on ALIMA's work in Africa. The voice-over for the campaign's lead video was by an African English speaker, so the vocal feel matched the footage and felt authentic.

Often what works in one country is taboo in another. I worked with a wonderful nonprofit that wanted to use its European campaign to expand its presence in the United States. The campaign wanted to include information in the form of an electronic "Green Book." Unbeknownst to them, in the United States, the *Green Book* was a travel guide used by Black Americans in the South during the Jim Crow era to show which places were safe to frequent. To use a "Green Book" would have been a turnoff to Influencers and parts of the audience that were seeking to engage. A different, non-controversial color replaced it.

> **Pro Tip:** *Always check slang before going out with public-facing content, or you may be embarrassed. I imagine the marketing managers for Ford autos were less than amused that their agency had not alerted them that Pinto, the name of their car, is slang for tiny male genitals in Brazil.*

Action Plan Step 4
Marketing Activations

Activation occurs when a marketing component of your Action Plan goes live. Include in your campaign plan which Activations you want to use, when, and how your Influencers fit in. Finding a specific day that fits your campaign—such as International Women's Day, National Doctors Day, or New York Restaurant Week—can be an excellent time to launch. On May 20, 2022, Entertain Impact released the album *Bangsokol—A Requiem for Cambodia* to commemorate the genocide that killed two million Cambodians, and to promote remembrance, reconciliation, and peace. May 20th was the Cambodian National Day of Remembrance for the genocide and an appropriate day to release the album. The arts are a powerful force to help heal and foster reconciliation in a post-conflict society.

Entertain Impact has built up a list over the years containing ideas of marketing Activations involving Influencers. We share these with our clients. There are dozens of choices, including hosting a gala or a panel, writing an op-ed, creating a petition, running a sweepstake, making a social media post, producing an online auction, creating a music video, making a congressional visit, and undertaking press interviews, a satellite tour or a town hall. The list is dynamic and is updated as new opportunities arise. You can find examples on the book's website.

> ***Pro Tip:*** *If you undertake too many Activations, none get done well, on time, or on budget. Don't cram in too much or be too broad. Less—and focused—is the approach to take for success.*

Consider the ratio of amount of effort to return when looking at each Activation, and ask yourself how it ties in with your goals as well as the degree of difficulty of getting an Influencer involved. An in-person live gala featuring an Influencer as the honoree, talent, or master of ceremonies requires many months of planning and upfront costs. An online gala where you deliver a bottle of wine and meal to each participant who then watches your star-studded show via Zoom may raise less revenues but net more income. It is also easier to get an Influencer to record a video than appear live at an event, although the latter is more of a draw. Likewise, a Multi-Pact is more complex to put together than a company simply hiring an Influencer for an ad campaign. Yet, the benefits from a Multi-Pact can be far more significant.

Know Your Influencer's Platforms

Your campaign marketing should drive your audience to one place to learn more, to give their contact information, and to take action. While creating your Action Plan, do research to ensure that your Influencer has a strong following on the platforms you want people to go to. Influencers posting on social media is the most common and cost-effective marketing tool to reach the maximum number. Suppose Selena Gomez posts on Instagram. A substantial portion of her 245 million followers will see it, and the cost per thousand impressions (CPM) will be minuscule compared to a traditional advert.

Each platform has a different audience. Choose your Influencer according to your target audience and the platforms they frequent. Here are a few over-generalizations:

- Facebook is for grandparents connecting with their grandchildren
- Twitter is for newshounds, academics, and opinion leaders
- LinkedIn is for business
- Clubhouse for techies
- Instagram and YouTube for everyone under forty-four years old
- TikTok for everyone under twenty-five years old.

An often-neglected platform is your email list. Influencers make people open your email. If the subject line says, "Ariana Grande gives," "Kanye West wears," or "Awkwafina stands up for," the Influencer Effect kicks in, and your open rate will likely increase. For my former client the Environmental Defense Fund, the most successful donation solicitation at the time featured the late Senator John McCain, followed closely by a polar bear.

Millennials, Gen Z, and Gen Alpha must put up with an overwhelming deluge of political, religious, and social propaganda on their social media. By engaging the appropriate

Influencer(s), you will stand out from the flotsam and jetsam attempting to reach the same audiences as you are. More than that, the quantity and quality of followers that Influencers bring to any campaign, as you will see later, boost your chances of achieving your goals.

ACTION PLAN STEP 5
Measurement

If you cannot measure something, then it is invisible or, at best, amorphous. That's why chapter 6—Step 5 of the D.R.E.A.M. process—is devoted to measurement of your campaign and the Influencer Effect. Identify your key performance indicators (KPIs) in your Action Plan and establish a baseline measurement. This gives you a benchmark to compare your actions against. KPIs are criteria that you can measure to assess your progress on your campaign such as money raised, goods sold, or brand awareness increases.

ACTION PLAN STEP 6
Set a Budget and Create Your Work Plan

Create Your Budget

This is where reality bites. You may have big D.R.E.A.M.s, but do you have the economic means to pull them off? With a bit of creativity, pragmatism, and discipline, the answer may well be yes. I have provided examples of realistic budgets with contingencies at goodinfluencebook.com.

One item you don't need to pay for in philanthropic campaigns is Influencers. If your research is good and you find people with authentic connections to your cause, they will almost always donate their services and keep expenses, if any, to a minimum.

Free is not always free, though. Don't forget travel, accommodation, and per diems. When an Influencer donates their services, there can be associated costs involved. For one Global Citizen concert in Central Park, all the artists performed for free, but there were still the cost of shipping their equipment, travel and hotel expenses. The trick is to make sure that expenses are known, contained, and reasonable. That said, most Influencers I have worked with have been cognizant of cost limitations when working with a nonprofit and do not ask for the same things they would if they were involved in a commercial project. I will go into how to control these costs in later chapters.

An Influencer fee for commercial campaigns can range from thousands of dollars for local campaigns to hundreds of thousands or even millions of dollars for national campaigns. However, when a brand integrates with a cause, Influencers will typically work for a fraction of their fee, or in exchange for a donation being made to their nonprofit of choice.

Make sure to look at the budget regularly, compare actual costs to budget, and make adjustments as you go along depending on your Influencer situation and the Activations you choose to do.

Create a Work Plan

Your work plan breaks down the Action Plan into small, identifiable tasks. Each entry shows what needs to be done, who is responsible, and dates. A one-line description can be helpful, but I wouldn't put more than that in the work plan. Keep it simple. I have seen work plans with a budget cost next to them and, on rare occasions, how much time is allocated to the task. I have also seen plans with the first tab showing the overall work plan and the subsequent tabs each representing a month with the calendar entries for that month set out. The section of my work plan devoted to Influencer engagement for a campaign, not the campaign overall, may look something like this:

Work Plan: Influencer Engagement

Undertake research batch #1 by July 3—Entertain Impact

Submit research batch #1 to the client by July 6—Entertain Impact

Client approves Influencer list by July 9—Client

Research Influencer contacts by July 11—Entertain Impact

Create Ask Letter and social media tool kit by July 12—Entertain Impact

Submit Ask Letter for client approval by July 13—Entertain Impact

Ask Letter approval by July 20—Client

Start outreach to Influencers by July 14—Entertain Impact

Engage Influencers by September 14—Entertain Impact and Client

Campaign launch by October 1—Entertain Impact and Client

Having the discipline to stick with your work plan keeps your project on track, on time, and under budget.

Establish Your Marketing Calendar

While a work plan operates on a micro level, a marketing calendar functions on a macro level. It covers a timeline of the key dates, events, and marketing activities important to your campaign. Usually, the marketing calendar is for an entire year and may include not just your campaign but other marketing activities.

Public anniversaries, celebrations or commemorative days can also be significant. If your campaign is on racial justice, Black History Month, MLK Day, and Juneteenth can be calendar dates to hang campaign activities around. Each campaign calendar is unique, but every campaign has one thing in common: they all list campaign launch dates.

Create Your Social Media Calendar

Tie your social media calendar into your overall campaign work plan and marketing calendar. This calendar shows what and when you will post content, and who is responsible for both. Scheduling posts saves time in the long run and helps keep posting consistent.

> **TOP TOOLS**
>
> *Social media scheduling tools help make posting easy and keep your calendar on track. Entertain Impact uses Buffer to schedule posts for the month. Scheduling posts saves time in the long run and helps keep posting consistent. Other tools that do this can be found on the book's website.*

Get Your Action Plan Approved

Your Action Plan is completed, contains a formidable campaign, and you are itching to get going. Now you will likely need final approval to make your campaign a reality. One of the most common mistakes in achieving this is to ignore the buy-in required from key decision makers. Many an Action Plan has laid dormant on the rocks of inertia because the decision makers were taken for granted.

My recommendation is to make sure your stakeholders know and feel invested in the Action Plan as it is being created. Then if you need to present the finished Action Plan, it's more a question of whether or not they buy into the Action Plan's approach and cost rather than the concept itself.

Stakeholders are people or groups that are interested in or can be directly or indirectly affected by your organization's actions. Make sure you cater to each group's needs and wants for any campaign. They include:

- For business: shareholders, employees, and customers
- For nonprofits: donors, supporters, and clients
- For both: regulators, policymakers, and communities

At this stage, create an executive summary with graphics and present it to everyone you need to support the project. I have been in this position several times on behalf of clients, and in all cases, the organization has moved forward, with only one exception. My worst experience in this regard was with a nonprofit where the chief marketing officer and head of its foundation hired me to tie Influencers into a major capital campaign. After months of work, I created an Action Plan that had the potential to accelerate fundraising enormously. Unfortunately, my team never got the opportunity to implement the plan because the two executives had not pre-cleared it with the organization's chief executive officer. It turns out that in a five-minute meeting that I had not been made aware of, let alone invited to, the CEO expressed his anxiety that a celebrity might cause a problem, and refused to implement the Action Plan. Not only was this a huge disappointment and the catalyst for introducing a needs assessment into my work, but by my conservative estimate based on experience with similar campaigns, this decision cost the organization over one million dollars in earned media value and tens of millions in donations that they could have raised, had they gone forward with the plan.

Having an Action Plan that is approved and ready to go is a huge thing. The road in front of you is defined, planned, and transparent, and you rightly feel all the excitement and optimism of the journey ahead. The next step is to research which Influencers you want to accompany you on this glorious journey.

CHAPTER 3
STEP 2: RESEARCH RULES

Life is a test many quest the universe, and through
my research, I felt the joy and the hurt.
—GZA, "B.I.B.L.E. (Basic Instructions Before Leaving Earth)"

O NE OF THE MOST ENJOYABLE and meaningful campaigns I worked on was Rotary's hugely successful "End Polio Now" campaign that engaged over eighty Influencers as Rotary Polio Ambassadors worldwide. Rotary, through this campaign, has raised hundreds of millions of dollars, vaccinated hundreds of millions of babies, and with other partners, ended polio in much of the world.

After Mel Gibson donated $1 million to the campaign, Rotary considered approaching Mel to join Influencers like Desmond Tutu, Queen Noor, and Bill Gates as Rotary Polio Ambassadors. As always, I researched Mel and found reports of his anti-gay and anti-Semitic slurs. I regretfully but strongly advised against Mel's involvement in the campaign. Fortunately, Rotary listened. Shortly after that, Mel was recorded making a very abusive and racist phone call with then-girlfriend Oksana Grigorieva.

Over the more than five years of "End Polio Now," that I oversaw all Influencer aspects of the campaign; no negative incident arose from any of the Rotary Polio Ambassadors. Why? In large part, it was due to excellent research.

Informed, in-depth, and current research will dramatically improve your chances of finding and engaging the right Influencers for your campaign and simultaneously minimizing risk. Quality research saves you time and money, and considerably reduces your stress level.

> **PRO TIP:** *Research every Influencer no matter how well you think you know them.*

Three Criteria for Vetting Your Influencer

For any Influencer, three primary criteria determine if they are a good fit for your campaign.

Relevance

Do they have a real relationship to the cause or brand? An Influencer should have an authentic connection to the issue they're elevating either because they have first-hand experience of the issue itself, or simply because they are already personally committed to the cause. Michael J. Fox is associated with Parkinson's research; Ricky Gervais, animal welfare; Elton John, AIDS research; Angelina Jolie, refugees; Rihanna, education and climate; Gary Sinise, veterans; Billy Jean King, LGBTQIA+ and women's rights; and Oprah Winfrey, education.

Reach

Do they reach your target audience? Beyond the total number of people, it's important to consider who exactly is being reached and whether that audience aligns with one or all of your desired audience segments. Laverne Cox, Miley Cyrus, Lady Gaga, Kate McKinnon, Tyler Oakley, Megan Rapinoe, and Wanda Sykes, all connect with the LGBTQIA+ community.

Resonance

Will they influence your audiences about your particular issue? A general ability to influence pop culture doesn't always translate into influence on a specific topic. You have to consider an Influencer's ability to deliver your message in a way that resonates with your target audience. Michael Phelps is a sufferer and spokesperson from depression; Alicia Silverstone is an animal rights activist; and Emma Watson supports women and girls' empowerment.

Classifying Influencers

Breaking down your Influencers by categories can help you think about how and where to do your research. There are a few ways of categorizing them, but the one most widely used is by followers. This is a convenient way to make order out of the vast Influencer world. Conventional wisdom categorizes an Influencer as mega, macro, micro, or nano. However, remember that whatever category is used for convenience, Influencers are people, not commodities, and respect is paramount.

Mega Influencers

Mega Influencers are at the top of the pyramid with over one million followers. They are famous, seen across all media, and have a broad audience reach. Usually, mega Influencers are well known nationally and internationally. Engaging a mega is expensive. Cristiano Ronaldo, one of the largest megas with over 300 million online followers, charges up to $1 million for one sponsored post. These mega Influencers have teams around them and numerous brand endorsement deals. To be involved with them makes your campaign highly visible and prestigious. Mega Influencer's followers, as a percentage of the total, don't generally heed a call to action as strongly as other Influencer categories.

For nonprofits, a mega may post gratis if they have an authentic connection. On behalf of March of Dime's "World

Prematurity Day" campaign, I reached out to Kim Kardashian, although we had never dealt with her team. Kim had a premature baby. They responded generously with a gratis post on her Instagram about the campaign. This would have cost over $100,000 if it had been a paid placement. For megas, the engagement rate is between 1 percent to 3 percent, so an authentic connection to your campaign is crucial, or you will not get the results you anticipated. Engagement rates will be higher if your research is good and your campaign well-executed. That said, engagement from even a small percentage of a large audience can yield big results: 2 percent of Kim Kardashian's 236 million followers is over four and half million people.

Macro Influencers

Macro Influencers have between one hundred thousand and one million followers. Journalists, activists, and media personalities tend to be over-represented in this category. Usually, macros have grown their audience online and nurtured a strong relationship with them. Audiences tend to be national but are also often international. Macros can reach broad audience segments such as young females, soccer fans, or millennial parents.[22] Macros are a category I like a lot. Macros generally have strong bonds with their followers, one specific topic area, professionalism, and easily identifiable relevance to your campaign. Making sure a macro is the right fit is vital.

---

22. Ismail, "Social Media Influencers"

Their audience will take action only if your campaign fits within the macro Influencer's subject area. A good friend of mine Esther Perel is a leading expert on relationships, who has rightly graduated from a Macro to a Mega Influencer. Anything Esther says on the quality of a relationship is taken seriously and received enthusiastically. Still, Esther is careful not to stray from her topic area. If Esther suddenly started giving cooking tips outside of the context of relationships, many of her audience would not follow her into the kitchen. Make sure your campaign is a good fit for your macro, or you will waste time and money. The good news is that engagement rates usually run around 3 percent to 5 percent.

Micro Influencers

With between ten thousand and one hundred thousand followers, micro Influencers make up the most crowded category. Generally, micros are subject matter experts, thought leaders, or industry experts. National and international followings are not uncommon. While they may have fewer people following them, their relevance to the subject matter is high. Suppose a resort in Mexico wants to attract tourists. Travel blogger Frenchman Pierre Schuester who has sixty-seven thousand Instagram followers would produce better results than a Mexican singer with five hundred thousand followers. Another advantage is that the costs for micro Influencers are lower than mega or macro Influencers. Engagement rates can run as high as 6 to 8 percent.

Nano Influencers

Nano Influencers are usually local community-based individuals with fewer than ten thousand followers who will often accept products in return for a mention in a post. Nanos are readily available, know their audiences well, are genuine, and consequently, their audiences take action at a higher rate. With nano Influencers' audiences, engagement rates can be as high as 10 percent or more, but their reach is limited. However, if you bundle multiple nano Influencers for a campaign, they can reach your audience and be a word-of-mouth driver. Take Dove, who launched Exfoliating Body Polish in Canada with fifty nano Influencers. Dover offered products and cash in exchange for the Influencer posting ads, adding links, and otherwise talking about the product to their followers. This approach allowed Dove to hyper-focus on an audience and create word of mouth or buzz about their product. With fifty Instagram posts by fifty nano Influencers, the total reach was 435,190. Their high 6.44 percent engagement rate resulted in over 28,000 engagements, at a low $0.14 per engagement. Not only that, but the audience was exactly the one Dove wanted to reach.

As a general rule, the engagement rate from an Influencer's followers decreases the more followers they have. While you get more active engagement rates as a percentage with a nano, remember that the total number of people involved is greater with a macro.

The number of followers—and the audience segment they represent—constitutes a significant factor in determining Influencer suitability. However, this is not the only consideration. You will learn about other factors later in this chapter.

A recent trend blurs the lines between a celebrity and a social media influencer. Many traditional celebrities have a massive presence on social media. And many social media influencers—previously only having broad reach on social platforms, now are crossing over to traditional media for exposure. Ziwe, Lily Singh, and Bella Porch are examples in the comedy and music fields who have made this crossover. That is why I use the term Influencer to encompass both.

> **Pro Tip:** *Get in early. Identify a future mega while they're still a micro by recruiting an Influencer early in their career. Manage the relationship right, and you and your Influencer can have a long and fruitful run together. UNICEF is particularly good at this. For example, they recruited Millie Bobby Brown from the show* Stranger Things *when she was only eight years old. She became the youngest-ever UNICEF Goodwill Ambassador at only fourteen years old. The actor is not just a Goodwill Ambassador in name. She presented at the organization's 70th-anniversary celebrations at the United Nations in 2016, its inaugural World Children's Day in 2017, and co-headlined with David Beckham at a United Nation's global summit to protect and promote child rights.*

Not all Influencers are human, or even alive! While this book primarily focuses on Influencers of the human variety, you should also consider Influencers of the non-human variety.

These might include artificial intelligence (AI) influencers, animals, celebrities dead but not forgotten, and even entertainment properties. More about those below.

AI Influencers

AI influencers are Influencers mainly in human guise, but created through artificial intelligence. AI Influencers have the advantage of being controllable, programmable, and teachable. Engagement rates are so far higher than in other Influencer spheres.[23] Lil Miquela, a "robot living in LA," has over 3.1 million Instagram followers, and Rozy, created in Korea by Sidus Studio X, has over 100 content sponsorships and is expected to earn over $1 million in 2021 for her owner. There may be downsides to AI influencers, such as whether their experiences are authentic, but do not be complacent. As we enter the metaverse,[24] AI is the next wave of Influencer marketing.

Animals

We all love animals, and many animals have the most popular social media followings. To support my client's "Canine Companions for Independence" campaign to raise funds and train free assistance dogs, I researched and reached

---

23. Zhang and Wei, "Influencer Marketing: A Comparison."
24. The metaverse is "an immersive virtual world where people gather to socialize, play, and work." Merriam-Webster Dictionary.

out to rescue dog Rusty Rodas. Rusty spread kindness and positivity to his nearly 100,000 highly engaged Instagram followers. His audience loved dogs and was passionate about dogs' abilities to make human lives better and happier (and vice versa). And, as a dog whose focus was to share joy, the campaign's messaging fit naturally into Rusty's brand platform and therefore resonated with his audience exceptionally well. As a result of Rusty and human Influencers, "Canine Companions for Independence's" fundraising goals were exceeded, and the organization increased their new donors at a higher rate than average.

Top animal influencers are usually cats and dogs and can earn their owners well over mid-six figures a year. Take award-winning canine celebrity Jiff Pom, one of the most followed animals on social media. A tiny Pomeranian dog with over 30 million followers across all platforms and A3 as its agent, Jiff makes appearances at corporate events, was a guest in a Katy Perry music video, launches e-games, and has released two shows and a book. Animals like this are cash cows for their owners, who charge significant money for one Instagram post. A recent phenomenon is agencies that only represent animals. Harvard-educated lawyer Loni Edwards founded The Dog Agency in 2015 after her dog Chloe, a Mini Frenchie, became an Instagram favorite. While a commercial endeavor, The Dog Agency does support animal welfare-related charities and issues. These agencies facilitate access literally to the top dogs in the industry, but it will cost you more than a dog biscuit. Depending on your campaign, an animal may be an appropriate Influencer. However, many animal welfare groups oppose this as a form of exploitation, so take potential political backlash into account.

Dead but Not Forgotten

There are also occasions other than Halloween where the dead do rise again! I once had a meeting with an agent about representing Albert Einstein for his philanthropy. Albert died in 1955; that's the year I was born. Just because a person has passed on doesn't mean they can't be an Influencer. Death may mean an Influencer's flame diminishes or shines even brighter across the decades. Certain iconic long-dead Influencers still have staying power and generate revenue for their estates. Albert Einstein, Gandhi, Marie Curie, Martin Luther King Jr., Mother Teresa, Che Guevara, Nina Simone, and Elvis were all worldwide Influencers in their day. Each has immense iconic potency today.

A movie, TV show, major event, retrospective, anniversary, or street naming can boost a dead Influencer. These visibility spikes make post-mortem Influencers more relevant to subsequent generations and increases their potency, reach, and earning power. For example, the 50th anniversary-release of The Beatles *Sergeant Pepper's Lonely Hearts Club Band*, the movie *Gandhi* winning the 1982 Oscar for Best Picture, and the Marie Sklodowska-Curie Award annual celebration has renewed focus on these giants and their achievements.

In the commercial world, Apple, with its 1997 Apple "Think Different" advert, benefited from the halo effect of the greats from across the ages. While costly, this advert campaign was incredibly effective in establishing Apple as a maverick brand by association. The upside of using deceased Influencers is that you know their reputation, but engaging them is complex and can be expensive for a commercial campaign. Agencies such as Greenlight represent the estates of deceased Influencers and are your initial point of contact.

Entertainment Properties

I have leveraged entertainment properties for philanthropic purposes for much of my career. I saw first-hand the power of music for social impact when I attended Live Aid in Philadelphia in 1985, where Jive artist Billy Ocean performed. That event and the movement raised awareness, millions of dollars, and the political will to fight poverty in Africa. That was followed by working on the #1 single "Self Destruction" by the Stop the Violence Movement, a group formed by another Jive artist KRS-One and Ann Carli, a colleague, to reduce violence in the hip hop community. My first Entertain Impact campaign consisted of an album, *Between the Covers*, and an accompanying TV show on VH1, which raised $360,000 for the T. J. Martell Foundation's cancer research. These and other music projects across the years proved to me how popular culture could create social change.

As powerful as music is, a major motion picture can change the hearts and minds of millions of moviegoers worldwide. By teaming up with a specific movie, you can reach a very targeted audience for a short period. In 2017, I brokered and executed a campaign with the Oscar-winning Pixar animated movie *Coco*. The movie is about a young Mexican boy who wasn't allowed to listen to or play music in his home. My client the Grammy Music Education Coalition (GMEC), consisting of over seventy educational organizations, had a mission to bring music to the 4 million public school students who had little or none in school. The GMEC campaign promoted the movie, and its central song "Remember Me" was performed by 200,000 students nationally and delivered the message that music is an essential component for children's education and well-being. In return, Pixar made donations to several music education nonprofits and sponsored an online classroom music teaching program. This partnership communicated the need for music in schools to the media, public, and local governments.

These various non-human partnerships, such as a movie or TV show, while not impossible to pull off, are challenging to consummate. My advice: stick with humans for now and then, as you build up confidence and expertise, consider these types of entertainment partnerships.

Choosing Your Number of Influencers

How many Influencers do you need to research? It depends on how many you ultimately want engaged in your campaign. An Influencer pipeline is the same as a sales pipeline and shows you the process you go through to get Influencers on board, e.g., the research, rejections, internal and client approval, and acceptance. Below is an example of a research pipeline showing each stage with the number of Influencers you might find in each:

Research (100)
Presented Internally (80)
Internal Approval and Outreach (60)
Influencer Accepts (8)

This pipeline shows the quantity and illustrates the conversion rates of prospective Influencers (100 > 80 > 60 > 8). Generally, I find that the Influencer acceptance rate is between 1:8 to 1:15, depending on the campaign and what's requested. Asking an Influencer to get involved on social media is easier than, say, an in-person visit to India.

Setting Your Timetable

Allow the optimal amount of time to do your research. You need to maintain a balance between having enough time to do the research thoroughly and not doing it so early so that it becomes out of date. Start your research eight weeks before you intend to reach out to any Influencers. This runway allows you to:

• Engage the right person to do the research. It may be you, an intern, or a paid freelance researcher.

- Agree on the characteristics and attributes you want to research, e.g., reputation, connection to cause, brands supported, and social media following. Place this information in a grid.
- Research Influencers across multiple categories to arrive at a list of Influencers that appeal to varied audiences.
- Review, refine, prioritize, and select your Influencers.
- Obtain approvals from your stakeholders, if needed.
- Collate contact information for each Influencer you decide to approach.
- Refresh your research on an ongoing basis.

You should have enough Influencer names at the end of this process to give yourself an excellent chance of success.

Identifying the Researcher

You may wonder who should do your research. A person (or several) educated on your audience and popular culture is the best choice to undertake your research. At Entertain Impact, in addition to our head of research specializing in Influencers and popular culture, there are over twenty independent vetted researchers with general and specialized expertise. They have their finger on the cultural pulse, in-depth knowledge of specific philanthropic areas, and can match the right Influencers to a cause. Often these tend to be young people who consume vast quantities of social media.

Preparing for Research

Creating a grid to track your research in a simple, succinct manner, giving only the pertinent facts, gets the job done. An Excel or Google spreadsheet with the column-headings below works, although you can add or subtract categories to suit your campaign:

- name
- professional name
- pronouns
- best known for
- occupation
- location
- cause connection
- philanthropy
- personal life
- reputation
- social media presence by platform
- additional notes
- recommendations
- client feedback
- next steps

I also keep a tab for Influencers who were initially considered but later determined not right. Perhaps they were not aligned with the campaign's ethos, or you had a reputational concern.

This list saves time and duplication down the line. You will find a sample grid on the book's website.

> **PRO TIP:** *Your initial round or two of research will reveal many appropriate Influencers. Track them on your grid. As your campaign progresses, do another round or two as you get feedback. This will uncover other directly connected Influencers since you are honing in on the essential factors for your campaign spokespeople. Also, during a campaign, I often read about a new Influencer interested in the cause I am working on and update my research to include them.*

Creating a Tiered System

With each campaign, I aim to assemble a cohort of Influencers of varying levels of public visibility, which I divide into three tiers. These tiers do not classify Influencers by mega, macro, micro, or nano or "A," "B," or "C" listers. As I stated earlier, I find these types of ranking can be demeaning and, frankly, not particularly helpful. Instead, my tiering system is based on the level of alignment—and hopefully involvement—that an Influencer will have in your campaign. Envisage it as a pyramid.

- Tier One Influencers are your champions. They are the ones who will be the most aligned with and involved in your campaign. They will provide your champagne moments and might be "big" names or more "niche." They may appear in adverts, contribute a quote for a press release, post on social media, make TV appearances, meet with policymakers, and participate in the in-house events for a brand or nonprofit campaign.

- Tier Two Influencers are your allies. It is great to have them involved, but they are not quite as aligned or as embedded as those in Tier One. A Tier Two Influencer may give in-depth support to your digital strategy such as providing an iPhone video for a donor event, posting unique or original content on social media for a brand campaign, or taking up an issue on Twitter.
- Tier Three Influencers are your supporters. While not your top picks or your campaign lead, you are glad to have them involved and appreciate their support. Usually, support at this level is social media lite, such as reposting key campaign content. Tier Three participants can, if nurtured, rise through the ranks and may become your most fervent Tier One champions.

Knowing the Criteria to Research

There are two stages of Influencer research. The goal of the first stage is to identify which Influencers have a connection to your cause or brand, and the aim of your second stage is to study each Influencer's individual attributes to make sure they are the right fit. Below are the main categories I research when looking at a particular Influencer. Some are qualitative—descriptive, conceptual, subjective—while others are quantitative—factual, conclusive, objective. The latter is easier to measure, but the former is equally crucial in informing your choices.

You can pick and choose the relevant categories for your current campaign. Usually, for any criteria that I believe could apply to any campaign, I will mark an X next to an Influencer's name on our research grid.

Here are the fourteen criteria to consider using for your Influencer research. While you can pick and choose from the menu, I have stressed which ones are essential for the Influencer Effect to be at its most potent.

Authenticity

"To thine own self be true" and "I'm real, I'm real, I'm really, really real" are lines from, respectively, Shakespeare's *Hamlet* and Kendrick Lamar's "Real."[25] Despite being 409 years apart, the message is the same: authenticity is a characteristic that we prize highly. We want to feel that the Influencers we follow are being honest and not trying to manipulate us.

The most critical factor in successful Influencer engagement in your campaign is an Influencer's authenticity. Please don't choose an Influencer simply because you personally are a fan or because they have a large social media following. Authenticity is the first requisite to creating a powerful Influencer Effect.

The Influencer's authenticity will extend to your brand or cause. We know from the myriad of academic and commercial research that an Influencer's authenticity positively affects

---

25. Used with permission. See Music Lyrics Acknowledgements for details.

consumer experiences and responses to brands. Pertaining to the commercial world, Michael Kamins and Kamal Gupta suggested that "the benefits of celebrity advertising may become increasingly more evident as the level of congruence between spokesperson and product image increases."[26] If the right Influencer is matched to the right product—or cause—the Influencer Effect can be powerful.

According to the 2015 research study "What Makes a Human Brand Authentic," the two main factors in the public's determination of authenticity are rarity and stability. Moulard, Garrity, and Rice, not a folk group, but the study's esteemed authors, define rarity as "the degree to which the celebrity is seen as uncommon." Mick Jagger is used in the paper as an example of rarity. Stability is defined as "the degree to which the celebrity is perceived as unwavering."[27] This approach is based on the idea that we are born with specific character-istics that do not alter over time. Tom Hanks, who is seen as straightforward and open, is a prime example of stability.

So, who do you think are the most authentic Influencers? The answer will depend on your age, since younger people value rarity and older ones, stability. Dave Chappelle, Hugh Jackman, Jennifer Lawrence, Lizzo, Barak Obama, and Ed Sheeran consistently rank as most authentic. You probably have your own list of inauthentic ones.

Authenticity is why George Clooney can advertise Nespresso coffee; *Modern Family* star Sofia Vergara, Head &

26. Kamins and Gupta, "Matchup Hypothesis Perspective," 569-586.
27. Moulard, Garrity, and Rice, "Makes a Human Brand," 173-186.

Shoulders; and Oprah Winfrey, Weight Watchers. Each one uses the product in real life. Oprah is so into Weight Watchers that she bought a stake in the company. When an Influencer has an ownership stake (e.g., Ryan Reynolds in Aviation Gin and Wrexham soccer club), authenticity is guaranteed, and they can be successful brand spokespersons. Shaquille O'Neal, a board member and franchisee of Papa John's, has been a big reason for that company's rebound. The Shaq-a-Roni pizza Shaq pitched also sold more than 3 million units and raised more than $3 million for charities in less than two months.

The reverse—inauthenticity—can lead to significant embarrassment. Diligent research would have avoided an uncomfortable situation for cosmetics company Yardley. They had signed actor Helena Bonham Carter to be the face of their company. Still, they had to end their relationship when Helena disclosed in an interview that she never wore make-up and had no idea why Yardley's had chosen her in the first place. Other examples of inauthentic behavior can play out over time. Certain Influencers who were promoting Samsung's Galaxy phone were then seen at the Super Bowl and Oscars using their regular iPhones. This rings—pun intended—of insincerity.

My favorite example of inauthenticity, though, comes from the unregulated world of social media influencers. In 2016, reality star Scott Disick was paid to promote Bootea, a weight-loss shake. The aim was for the public to believe Scott used the product organically, while in reality, he was being paid to post on his Instagram account. Unfortunately, Scott posted not only the post itself but also the instructions from the company: "Here you go, at 4 pm est, write the below. Caption: Keeping up with the summer workout routine with my morning @booteauk." Many of Scott's Instagram followers commented. Perhaps the most humorous was, "Bless you, Scott, not paid to think, just paid to promote." The trust level of Scott's audience plummeted because of his actions. As you know, trustworthiness is a crucial component to an Influencer being authentic.

Suppose your target audience trusts an Influencer who endorses a brand or cause. That trust will result in your audience paying attention and taking action in far higher numbers than they would without that certitude. Authenticity cuts through the tsunami of messages we are all bombarded with each day via the myriad platforms we follow. Ensuring an Influencer's authenticity when connecting them to your campaign is the primary factor in unleashing the Influencer Effect.

So, as you are doing your research, consider what the specific audience segment you are targeting considers authentic about any Influencer. Authenticity will impact whether you choose or reject a particular Influencer. When your audience genuinely believes in what your Influencer is pitching, your chances of engagement are dramatically improved.

> **Pro Tip:** *Adding a year or date range to your research question can help find more relevant and up-to-date information. For example, "Did Influencer X support Black Lives Matter from 2016 through 2020?" and compare that to the results to the question, "Did Influencer X support BLM only after 2020?"*

Reputation

After an authentic connection to your cause, the next crucial factor is the Influencer's reputation. Reputation is the belief that others have about a person's characteristics. Your Influencer may genuinely be of good character, but if the public, your board, or other stakeholders believe otherwise, for whatever logical or illogical reasons, then they are not the Influencer for you.

What makes up an Influencer's reputation? Depending on what is most important to you, you can create your list of attributes that you want an Influencer to manifest. Insight Timer, a meditation app, looks for meditation teachers known for their skill, compassion, and kindness. In contrast, sports brand Under Armour wants its brand ambassadors to be fit, serious, and driven.

Reputation is fluid, and it changes over time in response to the cultural pulse. In tandem, the public's goodwill towards an Influencer varies over time, so be aware of fluctuations. Our heroes fall from grace; some are resurrected, while others fail to recapture the public's love. Robert Downey Jr., Martha Stewart, and Lauryn Hill spent time in prison. After serving their sentences, they returned to the public's warm embrace and have had successful careers. The public tends to accept personal and self-inflicted criminal behavior, such as addiction, since they can relate to unfortunate circumstances and love a good come-back story.

Others do not bounce back. If there is even a whisper about your potential Influencer's involvement in—let alone conviction of—certain behaviors such as sex crimes, move on. Even if not convicted in a court of law, they will be found guilty in the court of public opinion and cast down forever from the mountain top of public adoration. Interestingly, specific crimes—such as domestic abuse—used to get a free pass and I wonder if certain male actors from that time would have had such successful careers in the era of the Me Too movement?

Reputation isn't just in the eyes of the media or the public, but also among the Influencer's industry colleagues. For example, there are on-set incidents of Influencers losing their cool over COVID-19 safety concerns or exhibiting unprofessional behavior to crew members. We all lose our cool, but these days, such incidents end up on social media in an instant(gram), impacting the public psyche. A quick online search shows the nicest as well as the most difficult Influencers. In the former category are LeBron James, Tom Hanks, Hugh Jackman, Dwayne Johnson, Jennifer Lawrence, and Gina Rodriquez. Oh, and the most difficult ones, you can effortlessly search for yourself.

> **Pro Tip:** *Be both general and specific in your search terms. A general search can give you the overview, and the specific term allows you to drill down on a particular facet. For example, searching for "What is an Influencer's marital status?" versus "Does the Influencer beat his wife?" will provide different information. The former reveals marital status and the latter marital discord.*

The saying "don't believe everything you read" applies ten-fold to the internet, so be cautious about what you take as gospel. When researching reputation, "scandal" is a search term that I use. Most searches return no negative results, or if there is a problem, the information turns out to be a total fabrication. Social media in particular is rife with fake and unsubstantiated rumors, gossip, and trolls. When Emily Blunt and Michael Bublé broke up, several unnamed sources stated it was due to Michael's infidelity. If you had stopped your research after seeing the original post, you may have disqualified Michael from being on your Influencer list. As it turned out, Michael needed to respond on social media to deny this fake story and preserve his reputation. Use caution, common sense, and fact-checking to verify or refute a social—or for that matter, a traditional media—story.

Ultimately, if your gut is that your potential Influencer's reputation is a poor fit with your brand, cause, or organization's culture, don't approach them. There are other choices, but if you do move forward, as you will see later in this book, there are safety measures to isolate you from this rare occurrence.

Geography

The geographical reach of an Influencer can factor into your decision-making. A few Influencers are known worldwide, from Accra to Zhenjiang and all places in between. These mega Influencers transcend cultures, generations, and languages.

Only for these elites will crowds in Tokyo or Rio di Janeiro wait outside a hotel for hours to get a sight of their favorite Influencer.

Other Influencers have a footprint across a specific country or region, but not materially beyond. Retired cricket legend Sachin Tendulkar is arguably the greatest cricket batsman the world has ever seen. His achievements are as, if not more, extraordinary than Michael Jordan, Simone Biles, or Tom Brady. Sachin is adored where cricket is a religion—India, Pakistan, Australia, England, South Africa, and the West Indies—yet he is largely unknown in the United States. Conversely, the reverse is mainly true in the case of US athletes in India.

The majority of Influencers cast a smaller geographical shadow. Local Influencers are the most plentiful, and the easiest to engage. There are likely several local Influencers in your city, town, or village (think the on-air news anchor, the college team coach, your local minister, or the CEO of your largest company). Despite having a smaller reach, local Influencers still motivate their local community. Take Lynda Smith, a local Arthur Murray dance school owner in Minneapolis-St. Paul. In 2010, Lynda started "Dancing with The Twin Cities' Celebrities" charity ball where local Minnesota celebrities perform with amateurs. In 2018, these local celebrities included Kate Perkins, a contestant on TV show *The Voice*; actor Erin Schwab; fashion designer Christopher Schwab; and fitness guru Melissa Duncan. This innovative event, sponsored by the Arthur Murray Dance Centers of Edina and St. Paul, has raised over $320,000 for the Leukemia and Lymphoma

Society[28] in honor of Jesse Smith, Lynda's late husband. This Multi-Pact has raised the profile of the charity and the businesses in the local community, all by creatively engaging very localized Influencers who are unknown to the majority of us. If you are a local organization, your campaign can be promoted by an enthusiastic and available Influencer from your community.

Language

The most limiting criteria for Influencer compatibility with your campaign is language. If I can't understand you, how can I connect with you? Influencers who only speak one non-English language will likely remain in their region even if followed by hundreds of millions of people. Take Johnny Hallyday, the French Elvis who sold over 100 million French-language records but was virtually unknown outside francophone countries. Halliday's death in late 2017 resulted in a nationally televised funeral, a guard of 700 motorcyclists, and a countrywide day of mourning in France. "Johnny was yours. Johnny was his public. Johnny was his country," said French President Macron. Yet, for most of the world, no one knew of or understood the significance of his passing.

By contrast, Columbian artist Shakira had the ambition, talent, and drive to break into English-speaking markets.

---

28. While the Leukemia and Lymphoma Society was the primary charity supported through this event, other smaller nonprofits also received donations.

Twenty-year-old Shakira, then a major Spanish language artist, learned English, wrote songs in English, and then recorded her fifth album, *Laundry Service,* in English. The album was released on November 1, 2001, and became a worldwide smash, selling over 13 million albums. Learning English resulted in many new opportunities and triumphs for Shakira. Among her accomplishments, Shakira performed the official Soccer World Cup song "Waka Waka" to a TV audience of over one billion people, earned numerous MTV and Grammy Awards, and became a worldwide Influencer.

Take into account the languages your audiences speak, and tailor your Influencer choices accordingly, but remember that much of the world speaks English, Mandarin, Hindi, Spanish, French, and Arabic.

Cultural Fit

When an Influencer is not aligned with the culture of your audience, stakeholders, project, or organization, you have an accident waiting to happen. Yet, finding the right cultural fit for multiple stakeholders can be a balancing act. I was engaged by Year Up to integrate Influencers into their campaign to reach disempowered youth in under-resourced areas like South Central and Compton in Los Angeles. Year Up facilitates internships and job training for high school graduates to help them secure careers so that they can leave behind minimum wage jobs or unemployment. Year Up had funding and didn't need to reach corporate America. Several recommendations of Influencers who would have reached Year Up's target audience—young people from these poorer LA neighborhoods—were rejected as likely to upset their corporate sponsors. However, after honing the research, other Influencers were approved, including NBA All-Star DeMar DeRozan, who grew up in Compton and attended Compton High School. DeMar supported the campaign with social posts. This example demonstrates the importance of the right cultural fit for all stakeholders.

Cause and Brand Connection

Even if you feel your Influencer is authentic, your research should uncover what other brands or causes an Influencer promotes to ensure they are congruent and not in conflict with yours.

Specific Influencers may have a singular cause they primarily support in the philanthropic world, such as Dolly Parton and literacy. Asking them to take on another cause would have a low chance of success. Others have several causes that they support. Usher has three pillars to his philanthropy: diabetes (as his son has type 1 diabetes), music education in schools in his hometown of Chattanooga, and youth development through his New Look Foundation. These are his primary focus. So, issues like heart disease, robotics, or Alzheimer's disease, despite being worthwhile causes, would not be the right match for him.

Other Influencers don't have one specific cause but are more theme or geographically focused. For example, Pitbull's philanthropy supports young people and education in his hometown of Miami. When your research uncovers a connection to an Influencer's passion, they will be more likely to support your cause.

Whatever Influencer you go for, it is essential that in your category, you have exclusivity, meaning other commercial sponsors, partnerships, or advertising arrangements do not conflict with, but compliment, your brand.

Finding an Influencer relatively free of related endorsements or philanthropic associations will give your brand or cause more credibility and potency. To do this, you need to either spot talented people and engage them when they are still young and starting their career, or else you need to find through your research that your Influencer of choice is not associated with any other brand or cause that would be in conflict with yours.

Location

Where an Influencer lives, comes from, or has a home will be a factor in your research. Often, these Influencers choose local charities and philanthropic events to support rather than national ones. After all, everyone is a local somewhere—even global celebrities! An under-utilized but constructive tactic is to research national Influencers with a local connection to your area. Perhaps they own a second home close by, or grew up in your town. Examples of local fundraising efforts by celebrities abound: Dave Chappell for his hometown radio station, Chance The Rapper for mental health services in Chicago, and Sandra Bullock for education in New Orleans have all been generous with their time and platform to raise money.

The Influencer doesn't need to be a mega to be effective. On the long-running soap opera *General Hospital*, actor Drew Cheetwood is Milo Giambetti, a bodyguard for a mobster and a stripper. He films in LA but loves living with his wife and three kids in Downriver, Michigan. Early in his career, Drew got involved with the Desi Geestman Foundation to raise money for families dealing with pediatric cancer: a local guy for a local charity.

Politics

A person's politics may matter for a particular campaign but usually do not. Generally, I take a non-partisan approach, find common ground, and embrace as many folks as possible, where possible. Both sides of the political spectrum came together in a campaign to preserve conservation funding in a farm bill that was in jeopardy of a veto from the George W. Bush administration. I secured a major music artist and environmentalist to have a private word with two Democratic senators, and NASCAR driver Ward Burton for a public meeting with Republican counterparts. Both Influencers from different sides of the political spectrum united around the need to preserve our public lands. Congress passed $4 billion of conservation funding.

Factor in politics when picking an Influencer if it will matter to your desired audience segments or stakeholders. Roseanne Barr, a far-right Trump supporter, will not influence a progressive audience unless you use reverse psychology and want them to do the opposite of what Roseanne is promoting.

Gender & Sexuality

Your level of research on gender or sexuality depends on the issue. Both gender and sexuality will have more relevance for an anti-LGBTQIA+ bullying campaign than saving the Brazilian rainforest. While specific causes are gender neutral, several have a gender slant. Traditionally veteran causes tend to be supported by men, and sexual abuse causes by women. However, don't restrict yourself to a particular gender. Incorporate outreach to the opposite gender and those who identify as gender-neutral or non-binary. Veterans' issues need women's voices, and for sexual violence to end, men have to be involved.

An Influencer's sexual orientation, or their sexual and gender identity—whether she, he, or them—plays a role in the public gravitating toward them. Some Influencers appeal specifically to men, or women, or other gender identifications along the spectrum.

If you use a gender lens, look at which audiences an Influencer turns on or off. YouTube entrepreneur Jeffree Star over indexes with a net approval of +14 among Gen Z women, but is -13 among Gen Z men. When Influencers like Ruby Rose or Sam Smith describe themselves as non-binary, they serve as role models to many young people struggling with gender identity. This identification makes them good candidates for LGBTQIA+ and human rights organizations. However, this declaration of identity will turn off many evangelicals who believe in the traditional male/female roles.

A person's sexual orientation is different from and not to be confused with gender. Your Influencer can identify as male, but their sexuality can mean they are attracted to men, women, both, or none. Your research needs to be clear in this area, should this be pertinent to your campaign.

> **Pro Tip:** *Pronouns matter. On your research tracking grid, always add the pronouns the Influencer uses—he/she/them. An Influencer's pronouns not only indicate gender preferences but let you know what to call them if you make contact. When in doubt, use they/them.*

Religion and Beliefs

How many times at award ceremonies have you heard the winners thanking God? An Influencer's faith, or lack thereof, informs much of their actions and willingness to engage with specific brands or social issues.

When trying to get certain Republican members of Congress to accept legislation on curbing carbon emissions, I employed the Christian stewardship of the Earth theology. This theology posits that God created the world, and humans have a duty to preserve it. To make this argument, I took Christian music artist Jaci Velasquez, and the president of the Trevecca Nazarene University Dan Boone, to visit Lamar Alexander, the then-senator for Tennessee. These Influencers had a positive affect on the senator, a man of sincerely held religious views, impacting his thinking on how Tennesseans felt about the topic and his approach to future legislation.

Touchpoint issues such as same-sex marriage will impact your Influencer choices. Suppose you are a company looking to reach LGBTQIA+ audiences, such as exemplars MasterCard or Target. In that case, you can discount support from those Influencers who believe that homosexuality is wrong for religious reasons. These would include passionate opponents, such as A&E's *Duck Dynasty's* Phil Robertson, a devout Christian suspended from the show for his anti-gay comments. Phil later rejoined the show, which subjected A&E to criticism from Faith Driven Consumer, a Christian group, for banning him in the first place, and GLAAD, an LGBTQIA+ advocacy group for choosing profits over gay people.

That said, there are many, if not most issues, where religion has no bearing. Most of us would not disqualify John Travolta, an avid pilot, from promoting a new flying product because he is a Scientologist. I have worked on healthcare initiatives such as polio eradication and diabetes prevention with ministers across the religious spectrum. These diseases are agnostic in that they affect everyone. Religion is not something that I usually research. Still, if you are involved with a Catholic medical charity or Mormon-owned business, you may need to factor this into your choice of Influencer.

Race

Race, ethnicity, and racial justice loom large in our national psyche and should play into your Influencer research. In the United States, racial justice as an issue reached a tipping point with the broader public after the killing of George Floyd, and the Influencer community responded. Tennis star Naomi Osaka used her platform at tournaments by adorning her COVID-19 mask with the names of Black people killed by police.

In countries where the population is not so diverse, aspects of ethnicity, not race, can still play a significant role. After the Rwanda genocide, I worked on radio ads narrated by Ziggy Marley to help bring Tutsi and Hutu together. For a vaccination campaign in India that aimed to appeal to Hindu and Muslim audiences, Bollywood actors were the commonality between these varied and vast populations.

> **Top Tools**
>
> *If you want to test how your audience will respond to a particular Influencer or campaign, you can run a focus group. Movie and packaged goods companies spend tens of thousands of dollars on focus groups. They will often reshoot parts of the film or redesign their label as a result. You can do this at a fraction of the cost by engaging your networks and running your own focus groups. Alternatively, use survey tools like PickFu. You can ask questions and get a preselected audience response for a few hundred dollars. I rarely use surveys to validate an Influencer but do so for key aspects of a marketing campaign, such as messaging.*

Age

One of the factors in choosing any Influencer is the age of the audience you covet. If you know YouTuber Like Nastya, you are not a rap fan but likely the mom of a young kid who subscribes to this channel created by the highly successful six-year-old girl. With over 75 million subscribers at the time of this writing—nearly five times as many as Lil Nas X—Like Nastya will get your message out to millennial moms. If you're a brand like Legoland, it will cost you a purported six figures to be in her video. Age is more than just a number. It is a robust connector to your desired audience. Specific Influencers such as Dwayne Johnson, or certain interest categories such as sports, do span across multiple generations, but most Influencers don't span more than one or two. A more viable and targeted approach is to adopt the rule that, with exceptions, an Influencer's age correlates approximately to the generation they attract.

There are generational differences in the effect that Influencers exert. YPulse's celebrity and Influencer survey showed that millennials and Gen Zs each gravitate towards a different category of Influencers. In broad brushstrokes, a musician is a better bet for a millennial. At the same time, a social media influencer attracts Gen Z. The virtual world has more power than the traditional world with the under-thirty-year-olds who allow more information on them into the public arena.

> **Pro Tip:** *Asking the same question in different ways yields different results. For example, "Where does Influencer X live?" or "Where does Influencer X have properties?" gets multiple results and connects the Influencer to other places.*

Relationships

Married or not, cohabitating or not, kids or not? There is no right or wrong answer. A person's relationships tell a lot about that person. Are they stable, erratic, or unpredictable? Are they estranged from their family, and if so, why? Larry King was married eight times to seven women, so long-lasting relationships did not rank highly. Alternatively, Elton John and David Furnish have been a couple since 1993. In his younger days,

Elton had numerous relationships, so people do change over time. While relationships may not be a vital component of your research, relationship status or stability may be relevant if your product, service, or cause is family oriented.

> **Pro Tip:** *Turn the page. Not all the best information is on the first page of your internet search results. Websites pay to advertise or improve their SEO (search engine optimization) to get a high page ranking. Turn the virtual page; otherwise, you will miss helpful information.*

Overexposure

If an Influencer is constantly seen everywhere, this can be a negative for any Influencer and brand. Ad-age has a list of the most overused celebrities in advertising.[29] A better way to look at Influencers would be to determine if they are effective for the brands, even if associated with several brands. The same can apply in philanthropy, where according to looktothestars.org, Sting is one of the most charitable Influencers supporting over 150 different organizations and forty-six causes. You have to decide when researching Sting if his generous association with so many other philanthropic organizations helps or hinders your cause, and the level of involvement from Sting you can expect.

---

29. Seattle Software Developers, "Most Overused Celebrities."

Getting the Message Out

Once you've completed your research on the Influencer's personal attributes, you can look at how they help you get your message out. Whether you are a casting agent, product manager, or NGO communications manager, you will want to know the reach of your Influencer through their social media and through traditional media.

Social Media Platform

Social media is a free, direct, and readily available means of communication to the public. There is no intermediary, and the Influencer controls it. Contrast this with traditional media such as newspapers, radio, or TV, where press coverage must be bought, earned, or donated. You certainly want your Influencer to earn traditional media placements, but that is not a given.

An Influencer's social media following is a strong indication of exposure. It's the number one quantitative data point. When looking at an Influencer's social media presence, there are various elements to assess: reach, impressions, engagement, content, and followers. You'll want to research these to help you decide which Influencer to pursue for your campaign. I define the five elements below with the disclaimer that this is not my area of expertise.

Reach

Reach is the number of people who actually see content posted on the Influencer's accounts. If the Influencer has 100,000 unique followers, and 30,000 of their followers see it, and then 15,000 of them share or retweet the post to all their friends and followers, the combination of their followers and other's followers is the Influencer's reach for that post. Check to see if the Influencers you are researching are followed on social media by other Influencers. If yes, this has the potential to help your brand or cause, as those Influencers may engage on a secondary level and thus amplify your campaign. For the African American Cultural Heritage Action Fund's campaign to preserve Nina Simone's childhood home, we engaged directly with several Influencers, including Mahershala Ali, Talib Kweli, Yusef / Cat Stevens, John Legend, Gregory Porter, Sonia Sanchez, Issa Rae, Sheila E., Anna Deavere Smith, Patti LaBelle, Gabourey Sidibe, Michael Bublé, and Kamasi Washington. Noname, a talented rapper out of Chicago, whom our research identified as citing Nina as one of her influences, took our campaign hashtag and turned it into #SaveNinaCrib. Several Influencers who followed Noname—including SZA, Smino, Barry Jenkins, Fashawn, Janelle Monae, Kehlani, Vince Staples, and Misty Copeland—then organically retweeted Noname and #SaveNinaCrib. Our total reach was doubled by other Influencers who followed the Influencers we engaged, and by media such as *AfroPunk* and *Paste Magazine* who picked up the story.

Impressions

The metric of impressions represents the number of times your content is displayed on a screen whether or not a user actually sees it or clicks on it. If an Influencer tweets twice to their 30,000 followers, then logically 60,000 is the number of potential impressions. However, if these two tweets are only seen by two-thirds of their followers due to Twitter's algorithm, the total impressions combined will be 40,000. Alternatively, if one tweet goes viral, it could be seen by, say, a million people. An Ellen DeGeneres selfie with a constellation of star actors at the 2014 Oscars was retweeted over 3.1 million times. All this to show: impressions are a moving target, although one that can be measured using the right software. Now, whether people view the content that is a different matter.

Engagement

Engagement is the number of interactions specific content receives from users, such as likes, comments, shares, or click-throughs. Likes comprise the largest proportion of the engagement rate, and comments, shares, and click-throughs will make up the remainder at a much lower proportion. For example, if a post with 30,000 impressions gets a 33 percent engagement rate, the activity on that post might be 9,000 likes and 900 comments, share, and clicks. The ultimate aim for engagement is to have your follower leave social media and perform your specified CTA (call to action), such as visiting your website, donating, or buying your product. So, if 30,000 people see a post and 3,000 people perform the CTA, the engagement rate is 10 percent.

Content

An Influencer may have millions of followers, but if the type of content they post does not resonate with your target audience, it matters little. If your campaign is outdoor-oriented and the Influencer is posting urban streetscapes rather than open vistas, pivot to another Influencer.

Followers

Beware of follower fraud. Genuine influencers build their following organically over time by posting a blog or YouTube video on a passion subject. Early adopters begin to follow them, igniting word of mouth, and their followers proliferate. Unfortunately, a rare number of Influencers will buy followers to make them look more popular, which helps them to make more money. In the music business I occasionally see artists who want to get signed inflate their numbers. If you are suspicious of any Influencers, ask the appropriate platforms to investigate, and in the interim, avoid that so-called Influencer.

> ***Pro Tip:*** *Be cautious if you think an Influencer doesn't have an organic following. You can tell through these signs:*
>
> • *Their follower acquisition graph looks like a hockey stick*
>
> • *Their engagement rate is well below the average for their number of followers*
>
> • *The presence of comments by followers that feel false, repurposed, or are out of sync with posted content*

> **Top Tools**
>
> *Several services can measure an Influencer's social media for free, such as Crowd Tangle, or for a fee, such as Union Metrics. Alternatively, you can do the research yourself. Suppose you are researching the social media followings of twenty Influencers. In that case, I'd suggest putting together a spreadsheet and populating it with the number of followers each Influencer has on each of their channels, which you can find by visiting their pages on each platform. You can also gauge the quality of fan interactions through the number of likes, retweets, and shares that any certain post has garnered.*

Traditional Media

You may have an Influencer on your list who fits many of your criteria, but who does not have a presence on social media. I reached out to Emma Watson for a social media post for a campaign, but Emma's social media was "dormant." In a case like this, consider if the Influencer has a presence through traditional media—this could help you with your campaign. Research in which publications your Influencers have appeared, and this will help you understand their potential to publicize your campaign and which audiences they reach.

Where to Research: Influencer Information Sources

The internet is your number one tool to get the information you need to find and assess suitable Influencer candidates. The freely-available online information is probably more than sufficient for most research purposes. Let's run through an example of finding Influencers who connect to a cause or brand.

For the African American Cultural Heritage Action Fund's campaign to preserve Nina Simone's childhood home in Tryon, North Carolina, the aim was to restore the house and talk about the African American historical narrative through preservation. For our research, we set two top criteria an Influencer had to meet: (a) recorded a song written or sung by Nina or been influenced musically by her, or (b) admires and respects Nina's civil rights activism. By asking the right questions, such as, "Which Influencers recorded or were fans of Nina Simone's music?" revealed a plethora of sources. These included Wikipedia, Lyrics.com, All Music. com, *People Magazine*, Spotify, and more. We also researched the movie and documentary on Nina and the accompanying tribute album to determine if participants could be potential

Influencers in the preservation campaign. All these and many other sources were free.

Sources to research Influencer attributes are numerous, easily accessible, and free. There are also several paid options which are more comprehensive than the free ones but can be costly. Unless your organization has a large budget, you'll probably stick to the free options. I recommend free, cheap, and paid options on the book's website, goodinfluencebook.com.

Top Tools

FREE

YouGov is a research firm that creates popularity and fame rankings for celebrities and Influencers. It shows how the public perceives Influencers and ranks Influencers, giving each individual Influencer a rating. For example, Miley Cyrus may be ranked number 1 in the pop artist category, but she is only number 128 in popularity. This ranking means that if Miley is your Influencer, you will get plenty of attention but less engagement. YouGov has accurate, easy-to-read presentation, valuable data, and rigorous methodology.

PAID

Celebrity DBI is a global Influencer evaluation service launched in 2006 that matches Influencers to brands based on key attributes. Celebrity DBI is easy to use, visually engaging, and you can get audience segment breakdowns. Limitations include the low total number of celebrities tracked (7,000), and at $20,000 per year, the fee is too expensive for smaller companies and nonprofits.

> When looking at any individual information source, whether free or paid, ask yourself if the information is reliable. Each source varies in depth, accuracy, readership, customer base, ease of use, customer support, number of Influencers, and costs. When undertaking your research, no single source is comprehensive enough. Look at several sources and cross-reference the information on the Influencer you are checking out.

> **PRO TIP:** Keep a master list of research sources, such as websites or articles that can be used any time you undertake Influencer research projects. This makes renewing or refreshing your research simple and fast.

Making Your Choices

You have done your research, and now you get to choose who you want to represent your brand or cause. I have a few tips to help you with your picks.

Don't Be Starstruck

When I ask my clients for Influencer suggestions, invariably they name mega Influencers. You must ask yourself, "Are they suitable for what you are looking to achieve?" If, say, you're trying to reach women ages eighteen to twenty-five, YouTuber and TV host Ziwe Fumudoh may be a far better choice than, say, Julia Roberts. Don't let famous names cloud your judgment. Match the right Influencer to the right audience. If in doubt, swipe left and move on.

Broaden Your Criteria

Please don't make your Influencer criteria too narrow. Otherwise, you severely restrict your ability to get Influencers on board. When I worked with a prominent New York nonprofit on their fundraising campaign, they were initially highly conservative in their criteria for choosing Influencers. These restrictions limited the size of the potential Influencer pool, and their cause did not garner much initial interest. However, once the executive team relaxed its criteria while still being true to itself, the tide turned, and several prominent Influencers came on board. The campaign raised a then-record amount to fund its programs.

Be Spoilt for Choice

There are significant advantages to having several Influencers for your campaign.

Avoiding Reputational Risk

Having only one Influencer as your spokesperson leaves you vulnerable. Your campaign can be damaged should that

Influencer misbehave. Perhaps the most precipitous fall from grace in sports was seven-time Tour de France winner Lance Armstrong. The Lance Armstrong Foundation, the juggernaut cancer research charity founded by Lance, had revenues of $41 million in the year he came back from retirement. After news of his use of performance-enhancing drugs, they plummeted to $2.5 million. The Foundation nearly went bankrupt, sold its headquarters, and rebranded the entire organization to Livestrong in order to survive.

The consequences can be dire for brands if their only Influencer's reputation is damaged. Take Jared Fogle,[30] who attributed his 200-pound weight loss in large part to his Subway diet and became their spokesman for over a decade. The company attributed over one-third of its revenue during that period to Jared's involvement. This rosy picture changed dramatically when Jared was convicted of sex crimes in 2015. He is now in prison. Had Subway had other spokespeople at the time, they could have mitigated the fall-out from this scandal. However, according to international research data and analytics firm YouGov, Subway's brand reputation recovered within a year.[31] My approach to avoid a similar fiasco on the rare occasion that an Influencer makes a faux pas is to have several others in good standing left to promote the cause and maintain reputational integrity. There is safety in numbers.

Should this happen to you, circumstances will dictate if you divorce from your Influencer in public or private. In

30. Murray, "Subway Commercial Spokesman."
31. Wong, "Subway Sales."

2009, Kellogg consciously uncoupled from Michael Phelps, the most decorated Olympian of all time, when a photo of Michael smoking marijuana was leaked. Despite a public apology, Kellogg spokesperson Susanne Norwitz stated, "Michael's most recent behavior is not consistent with the image of Kellogg. His contract expires at the end of February, and we have made a decision not to extend his contract." Later, Michael redeemed his reputation by being open about his mental health issues and how therapy "saved his life." This led to a brand partnership with online therapy provider Talkspace, where Michael talked about mental health stigma and ways to get treatment.

In my fifteen-plus years of working with Influencers professionally, I have never had a reputational problem with any Influencer. I put this down to thorough research and, of course, a smidgen of good fortune.

Safety in Numbers

An additional benefit of being open to having several Influencers on board is that other Influencers are far more likely to say yes when you approach them if other Influencers have already agreed to participate. This is a chicken and egg situation. To mitigate this in part before we have an Influencer on board, I always let the target know which other Influencers we are going out to and that we have interest from several. This way, their reps feel more comfortable with reviewing my request.

Availability

Engaging several Influencers has other significant advantages. If you have only one Influencer and they are, say, shooting a movie, they may be unavailable for months. I learned this lesson when shooting a public service announcement for the American Dental Association's "Give A Child A Smile" campaign with baseball-great Albert Pujols. Albert played for the Saint Louis Cardinals. (un)Fortunately, Albert's team made the playoffs, and only after they were eliminated could I go ahead with the shoot. Having several Influencers gives you choices and won't delay your campaign.

Diversity

My other reason for promoting several Influencers is diversity, equity, and inclusion. Your research will reveal several Influencers, each appealing to a particular segment of your target audience. Selena Gomez, YoYo Ma, Drake, Celine Dion, Black Pink, A. R. Rahman, Ziggy Marley, and Taylor Swift are all musicians, and each appeal to distinct audience segments.

A 2019 study by YPulse found major differences between the type of Influencers that are most popular with millennials, Generation Z, and Generation Alpha. Millennials go for Hollywood actors, Gen Z for musicians, and Gen Alpha for online personalities. All three agree that politicians are at the bottom of the list.

For Rotary's "End Polio Now" campaign, the eighty-plus Rotary Polio Ambassadors came from every part of the planet. They were appealing to diverse audiences of every shape, location, and color of the human rainbow. For South Korea, a lucrative fundraising country, our research uncovered that both the father and grandfather of singer Psy of "Gangnam Style" fame were Rotarians. Psy, at the time the hottest star on the planet, agreed to participate in the campaign. The surrounding publicity was a major boost in South Korea and much of Asia for polio eradication.

I understand that budget is a consideration for a purely commercial project where the Influencer is paid. Yet, whenever feasible, having several Influencers is still preferable. Companies today may choose to spend their budget not on one major Influencer but rather on hiring several micro or nano Influencers to reach local or ultra-precise audience segments.

Ambassador Programs

I like ambassador programs. A cadre of Influencers connected to your organization and readily available to offer their support is a valuable asset. There are several factors to consider when creating an Influencer ambassador program:

Number: The make-up of your ambassadors and how they connect to audiences is a crucial factor. The American Red Cross has thirty-six diverse Influencers from music, acting, and sport who appeal to US-centric audiences over forty-five years old.

Qualifications: Notoriety, an authentic connection, and appeal to your target audiences are necessary. North Face, an outdoor recreation product company, has brand ambassadors who are all extraordinary athletes, such as ultra-marathoners and mountain climbers. These ambassadors are far more effective for North Face's audience than if they hired The Rock or Vin Diesel.

Term: A year is a reasonable length of time to get to know one another and for the Influencer to show a commitment to your brand or cause.

Activities: Ask the Influencer to agree to international field visits, media tours, event attendance, public advocacy, fundraising, and social media posts. This commitment over twelve months is the United Nations Goodwill Ambassador model, which has stringent guidelines for accepting anyone into their program. On the commercial front, clothing company Revolve has over four thousand social media influencers who get marketing support, a commission on any sales they generate, and entry to cool events.

Check Your Corporate Culture

When making your Influencer selections, it's essential to know your organization's cultural comfort level if you want your Influencers to be enthusiastically embraced. I recommend using what I call the front-page test. Basically, you ask yourself, "How would our board, major donors, stockholders, colleagues, employees, or vendors feel if a national newspaper ran a front-page story about our organization working with a particular Influencer?" If there is even an iota of doubt in your mind, nix that particular Influencer and move on. There are plenty of others who will be a better fit.

A stark contrast in Influencer support can be found by comparing PETA, an animal activist organization, and one

Chapter 3: Step 2: Research Rules   **143**

of my former clients American Humane, an animal welfare organization. PETA's edgy "I'd Rather Go Naked Than Wear Fur" campaign was embraced by supermodels, actors, athletes, and musicians, including Naomi Campbell, Tony Gonzales, and Melissa Etheridge. All took their clothes off to protest fur as clothing. By contrast, American Humane would recoil in horror at such an approach, preferring cooperation to confrontation. Its Influencers tend to be mainstream animal lovers like Kristin Chenoweth, Miranda Lambert, and the late Betty White. Both organizations do good work. The disparity between the two in their choice of Influencers is predicated upon different value systems. PETA vehemently believes that animals are "not ours to experiment on, eat, wear, use for entertainment, or abuse in any other way." In contrast, AHA wants to improve animal welfare but acknowledges that animals are eaten and appeals to a more conservative crowd. Both have positive outcomes.

Rank Your Choices

If you have researched eighty potential Influencers, you need to determine a priority system to guide your outreach plan. Which ones will you reach out to, and in what order? You may want to pick a target number of Influencers (e.g., the first twenty approved names), or use a ranking system. Here is an example of Influencer ranking for an animal welfare campaign using a scale of zero to ten points, with ten being the best and zero representing the worst fit.

Influencer A (240M followers)	Category Points
Celebrity Assessment	8
Cause & Brand Associations	6
Social & Traditional Media	9
Total Score	**23**
Influencer B (3.5M followers)	**Category Points**
Celebrity Assessment	10
Cause & Brand Associations	9
Social & Traditional Media	10
Total Score	**29**

Question: out of the two, which one would you choose? Influencer A would reach more people with their tremendous following, but Influencer B has better scores. Answer: rather than choose one over the other, select both and connect with each of their followings.

I like to keep it simple by using a red, amber, and green ranking system. Green being a yes, red a no, and amber a maybe.

Trust Your Gut

Choosing from the batches of Influencers you have researched is a process. Not everyone will be a perfect fit. The definite yeses and the rejects are easy. The maybes are where you can run into trouble. In these cases, listen to your inner voice. If you have an uncomfortable gut feeling about any potential

Influencer, cross them off your list. Greg McKeown's excellent book *Essentialism* reiterates this life lesson. For any decision, unless it's an absolute yes, it should be a no. Apply this to your Influencer choices, and you'll end up with the right selection.

How to Get Your Choices Approved

Presenting Your Research

Gathering information is one thing; presenting it to those who approve which Influencers to approach is another. Here, form and substance both count.

Judgment

When presenting Influencer research, I offer my opinion on which Influencers are the best match for a brand or cause. Likely, you will not know who all the Influencers are that you or a team member are researching, so assume the folks you are asking for approval will know even less. To that end, I like to put a priority system in place when delivering research that highlights those that I feel are the best choices for a particular campaign. I have seen complicated systems, but a simple green, amber, red, 1, 2, 3, or A, B, C categorization saves time and helps the decision turn out the way you want.

In-person Conversations

I have found that going through a list of Influencers with a client or my team prompts a fun and energetic discussion. Further, this debate is rarely confined to the list that we have presented, and serves as a catalyst for suggestions for other Influencers that are additive. So listen carefully, be open to suggestions, and you'll find some gems.

Batches

If someone hands me a grid with eighty Influencers, honestly, my eyes glaze over. To give these to your management or partners in one go can be overwhelming. I have found that providing the information in batches of twenty names is easier to digest and makes decision-making quicker. This method also allows you to reach out to Influencers on a staggered basis, rather than all in one go, making the process more manageable.

Under Promise and Over Deliver

My experience is that most people do not comprehend the sheer volume of requests an Influencer gets every day. Nor do they fully grasp the (un)likelihood of getting every approved Influencer, especially the megas, to say yes. Just because you think Tyler Perry is perfect for your cause doesn't mean that Tyler or his people will feel the same way. It is better to set expectations low to appreciate any wins over and above your baseline.

Rejection

Most of your recommendations will be approved by your client or management, but don't be disappointed if one or two are not. For the American Diabetes Association's "I Decide to Fight Diabetes" campaign, my research uncovered that Oscar winner Halle Berry had type 1 diabetes. Unfortunately, Halle's medical regime did not conform with the association's protocols, so I was not approved to approach her. Fortunately, Donnie McClurkin, Patti LaBelle, Sherri Shepherd, Maria Menounos, Donna Richardson Joyner, and Mama Love were approved and all supported the campaign. Each campaign or organization has its reasoning, culture, and idiosyncrasies. You need to respect them.

Refresh Your Research

An initial round or two of research will reveal many appropriate Influencers, but that may not suffice. As your campaign progresses, do another round or two of Influencer research as you get feedback from the campaign stakeholders. This will uncover other directly connected Influencers since you are honing in on the essential factors for your campaign spokespeople.

As your campaign may last several months, keeping your research up to date is important. Not only will Influencers' reputations ebb and flow, but a new Influencer may come onto the scene that is a perfect fit for your campaign. I often read about a new Influencer interested in the cause I am working on and update my research to include them.

Conclusion

The list of causes Influencers are passionate about is as long as the list of, well, causes. Match an Influencer with a cause close to their heart, and you have a champion connector. Now let's go get your champions.

CHAPTER 4
STEP 3: ENGAGE

You gotta cultivate what you need to need
—Sonic Youth, "Confusion is Next"

WHEN IT COMES TO INFLUENCERS, access is everything. You can't just text Drake or send a quick email to Jennifer Lawrence. You may not even know who represents them. But I do, and in this chapter, I'll share my industry insider knowledge on how to connect with Influencers and make your request stand out from the twenty others your intended Influencer already received that day.

Here's the good news: you are more connected than you think! There is a theory that any two people in the world are six or fewer people away from each other. You've probably heard of the six degrees of Kevin Bacon game. The aim is to link Kevin with any celebrity in six degrees or less. For example, Andrew Garfield was in *The Amazing Spider-Man* with Emma Stone, who was in *Crazy, Stupid, Love* with Kevin, so Andrew is two degrees away from Kevin, and Emma one degree away. While it started as a cult game, six degrees is now part of the vernacular with websites and apps.

Before I ever had contact with Kevin, I didn't know his manager, but an attorney friend did, so I guess I was three degrees away from Kevin. That was in 2004, and I wanted Kevin's band, the Bacon Brothers—formed with his brother Michael, the Emmy award-winning composer—to host my first-ever charitable Activation. The Activation involved a VH1 TV appearance to promote an album called *Between the Covers* consisting of cover versions by well-known artists such as Alicia Keys, Madonna, Mick Jagger, and David Bowie. 100 percent of the proceeds from the album went to the T. J. Martell Foundation for cancer research. The Bacon brothers agreed to host, donated their services, and performed the Beatles song "If I Needed Someone." VH1 produced the show pro bono, and the album raised $360,000 for HIV and cancer research.

The six degrees of Kevin Bacon game initially annoyed Kevin, but out of this discomfort was born SixDegrees.org, Kevin's nonprofit that "uses everyday activities to connect people to causes." Over the last several years, I have been fortunate to support Kevin in his philanthropy, along with Stacy Huston who heads up SixDegrees.org.

According to Facebook, each one of us is on average only 3.57 people away from everyone else—or at least from any one of their 1.5+ billion users. That means your friend's friend's friend's friend "is sufficient to link you to almost everyone in the world." This small distance means you have plenty of opportunities to employ the Influencer Effect by utilizing your networks. Painter Haley Mellin cofounded Conserve, a small, volunteer-run organization with a big mission to collect donations for global land conservation—acre by acre. Haley, mining her art world connections, formed a partnership with artist Zaria Forman, a macro Influencer. Zaria's photorealistic large-scale pastel drawings of glaciers document the impact of climate change and match Conserve's mission. Zaria's gallery Winston Wächter Fine Art joined to complete this Multi-Pact. The gallery donated a percentage of Zaria's prints to Conserve and raised the organization's profile with art patrons.

Before going into logistics of how to engage your Influencers, let's walk a mile in the shoes of one. Being an Influencer has many advantages, but the demands are enormous, and the scrutiny intense. Influencers get requests several times a week. Megas get them many times a day. I support several well-known actors and musicians for their philanthropy, and on average, they get eight requests a day, or nearly 3,000 a year, from all over the world. These requests are asking for their time, money, endorsement, and want them to travel locally or internationally, attend events, give speeches, make media appearances, and be in video shoots.

Imagine, for a moment, how you would feel if I asked you to take three days out of your busy work schedule, leave your family and fly three thousand miles round trip from LA to Lebanon, Kansas, all for free, despite you losing three days of earnings. That's a big ask. And why? To give a three-minute speech for a cause, company, or place you have no connection with. The likelihood is, you'd say no! If Influencers fulfilled only ten percent of the requests they received, their every waking moment would be consumed by philanthropy. Forget about working or seeing their family. Consequently, your approach needs to be well crafted and compelling to cut through the clutter.

Now, let's get into the logistics of making the Ask.

An Overview of the Ask

The Ask is an industry term for when you "Ask" an Influencer to do or donate something. Crafting an effective Ask is an art. You use the medium to present a compelling case for why an Influencer should give their time, reputation, and more to your cause or brand. The Ask is a manifestation of all your thinking and planning to date. To make a powerful Ask, you need a strong campaign with specific requests for what you want your Influencer(s) to do.

What Is the Purpose of the Ask?

The purpose of the Ask may seem obvious, but there are several benefits of making an Ask beyond getting an Influencer on board. You know the Influencer, but they may not have heard of your organization. The Ask educates your targeted Influencers and their representatives about your organization. If you want five Influencers for your campaign and you reach out to forty, there are probably one hundred people—between the Influencers and their representatives—who now know about your organization. Even if you get a no from the majority, you have established a dialogue and set yourself up for another request down the line. Through the Ask experience, you will know the right people to connect with and better understand how the entertainment ecosystem operates.

Personalize All Asks

Everyone wants to be loved, so a "To Whom it May Concern" generic email guarantees failure. Why? Because your greeting alone makes it obvious that the particular Influencer you're reaching out to is just one of a long list of names, and is very likely not your first choice. If you are only doing one or two campaigns a year, creating individual emails by hand is feasible, if laborious. Just make sure that you have the correct Influencer's name throughout the email, and if you cut and pasted, didn't leave the previous Influencer's name in one of the paragraphs by accident. To make the "by hand" personalized approach a little quicker, I usually save a version of the Ask letter as a template in Gmail. There are also software services that you can use to send out email Asks in bulk, like Mailchimp, that make each one look personalized. You can get more information on this and other programs on the book's website.

The Look

While a regular email will suffice, it will stand out from the pack and may get a better response if you spruce it up a bit. For ALIMA's "Oxygen for Africa" campaign Ask, we put a branded banner in the header of the email. As Andra Day's manager Jeffrey Evan's said to me, "If there is a graphic on an Ask, I treat it more seriously." However, I wouldn't agonize over this. In most cases, a regular email will do the trick.

Short and Sweet

Given that Influencers and their teams are inundated with requests and have short attention spans, your Ask should be no more than a page long. So, be succinct when introducing your organization, cause, and request. The Ask letter is an invitation for a conversation, not a short story, so over-detailed and extensive Asks are not optimal for success.

Materials

Try to avoid attachments to your Ask since they can cause your email to get blocked by a spam filter. If there is a need to include an attachment, keep it as simple as possible and preferably send them as links. My preferred attachment is a link to a social media kit or a one-pager infographic. Where possible, to save time and money, use or adapt existing in-house materials.

Date

If you need an Influencer to be somewhere or to make a post on a specific date, say so when you make your request. Ambiguity leads to stress and failure. Bear in mind that setting a particular date reduces your chances of success since the Influencer may not have availability, although you have no choice in the case of an event. Whenever you can set a date range of a few weeks, this improves your Influencer's ability to accommodate your request. Generally, setting deadlines or date ranges helps get responses and is more efficient.

Components of the Ask

The essential components of the Ask establish who you are, why you are making the request, what you want the Influencer to do, where the Ask will take place, and when the Ask needs to be completed. Let's break down the Ask into its component sections using an example from a campaign for the World Health Organization Foundation called "Go Give One." This campaign was dedicated to vaccine equity, and since this was not yet a well-known topic, the Ask was longer than usual, as it required additional explanation.

Subject Line

Create a subject line that catches the eye and makes the reader want to open it. For example, "Invitation for (Name) to Support Vaccines for All with the World Health Organization." This way, the Influencer knows what the email is about from the subject line alone.

Introduction

Start the Ask letter with a brief introductory paragraph about the campaign. This way, the reader gets an executive summary of all the information. For example, "We are reaching out to invite (Name) to support the Go Give One campaign, an international campaign created by the World Health Organization Foundation supporting global COVID-19 vaccine equity."

Set Out the Problem

You need to educate the Influencer on the problem your campaign addresses. For example, "Less than 2 percent of people in low- and middle-income countries have been vaccinated against COVID-19. Expert forecasts indicate that the world's ninety-two poorest countries will not be able to vaccinate 60 percent of their populations until 2023 or beyond. In stark contrast, high-income countries have enough doses to vaccinate their populations more than twice over. This means COVID-19 will be with us worldwide for years to come."

Explain Your Campaign

Educate your target influencers and their representatives on your campaign. Briefly describe your campaign and include a link to your website, social media, or video content if they exist. This way, the Influencer gets a sense of the quality of the campaign. For example, "Go Give One seeks to achieve vaccine equity by raising money for COVAX, the international COVID-19 vaccine sharing program. COVAX is currently underfunded and has struggled to meet its vaccination targets. To help combat this, Go Give One is asking individuals to donate $5, the cost of a vaccine."

Your Organization

Be very specific about your business or nonprofit so that the Influencer feels comfortable. For new organizations, so long as your mission resonates with the Influencer—whether to make the best jewelry from sustainable materials or fight poverty in the USA—and has a website or other evidence to back up its veracity, the representatives will probably be satisfied. As name recognition of the World Health Organization is high, I didn't need to explain who they were in the Ask. Still, if I did, I would have added, "The World Health Organization Foundation raises money and grants to support the WHO's efforts to provide health care, emergency aid, and universal health coverage to the world's vulnerable populations."

Special Circumstances

If part of your campaign has a hook that you feel will help an Influencer say yes, then include it in your Ask. For example, "We're excited to share that the ELMA Vaccines and Immunization Foundation has agreed to match up to $1 million in donations to Go Give One. To help reach this goal, we are asking people such as (Name) to help raise awareness about the campaign."

Who Else?

An Influencer is far more likely to say yes if other Influencers have already agreed to participate in your campaign. This is a chicken and egg situation. To mitigate this in part before you have an Influencer on board, I always let the target Influencer know which other Influencers are being approached and who has expressed interest. There is safety in numbers, which makes their reps feel more comfortable when reviewing my Ask. For the "Go Give One" Ask, I wrote, "From the stage of the recent Global Citizen concerts, the Duke and Duchess of Sussex and Priyanka Chopra supported vaccines for all, and Sir Elton John explicitly endorsed the campaign. To support this campaign, we are also reaching out to several more influencers, including Selena Gomez and Viola Davis."

Request

Every Ask should have a specific request. The Ask will depend on which tier your Influencer occupies. Try not to ask for too much initially since this can overwhelm the Influencer and turn them off. You will be more successful if you specify one or two things at most. As your relationship grows, you can make additional Asks. It is important that you set out clearly what you are asking the Influencer to do. For example, for "Go Give One," the request to the Influencer's representatives was as follows:

> Based on (Name's) history of advocating for COVID relief, we believe their voice would be a significant addition to support this campaign and help promote the $1 million match to buy 400,000 vaccines. If (Name) is interested in supporting this vital initiative to save lives, please find a social media kit that can be used to support the campaign in the coming two weeks beginning on Z date. Thank you so much for considering this important initiative.

Response

It's wise to repeat at the end of your Ask the best way for the Influencer or their representative to respond to you. Keep it simple, along the lines of: Please feel free to reach out to me at (add your email) with any questions. And thank you for your consideration.

Types of Asks

Social Media

Currently, the majority of Asks I make have a social media component. The social media kit is an attachment or a link to materials containing messaging, graphics, a posting calendar, a tracking link, and other relevant details. For a social media Ask, you have two choices: (1) wait until the Influencer says "I am in" and then send a link to your social media tool kit, or (2) send a link to the kit with the initial Ask email. I prefer sending the kit with the Ask. It reduces the back and forth and can easily be forwarded to the Influencer or their social media manager to review. You'll find an example of a social media tool kit on the book's website.

Appearance

The other Ask types primarily involve asking the Influencer to make some sort of appearance, such as be in a video, visit an organization, go on a trip, or attend an event. Provide details of the event, location, date, and outline what the Influencer will do. An assignment that combined my passion for music and philanthropy was engaging musical talent for the 2022 Skoll World Forum at Oxford University. The Ask explained that the conference focused on social entrepreneurs and described the attendees (socially conscious companies, non-profit leaders of civil society, and social entrepreneurs), and the request was for a 20-minute performance at the award ceremony. The notable Benin artist, multiple Grammy winner, and UNICEF Goodwill Ambassador Angelique Kidjo confirmed, but due to COVID, the 2022 Forum—including Angelique's performance—migrated online. Angelique and Skoll were a perfect fit for each other. Angelique's music both entertains and provides a platform for social change. In 2006, Angelique created the Batonga Foundation that equips the hardest-to-reach girls and young women on the African continent with the knowledge and skills they need to be agents of change in their own lives and communities.

I was also fortunate to engage actress, teacher, playwright, and author Anna Deavere Smith for the 2022 Skoll World Forum. Anna's work—*Twilight: Los Angeles* through *Notes from the Field*—created a new form of theater that looks at current events through journalistic interviews interpreted through performance. Social justice and art combine in a powerful way through Anna's ability to present a cohesive play containing multiple narratives. Last but not least, the blind Malian singers and musicians Amadou and Mariam appeared at the 2022 Skoll World Forum. Their work not only within the blind community but also for the World Food Program and End Water Poverty have made them part of the artist activist community.

Any visit is a significant Ask, especially an international trip since it involves spending time, resources, and money. The return had better be worth it. That said, the awareness and publicity can be substantial. I have worked via ELMA Philanthropies with Saint Damien Pediatric Hospital in Haiti cofounded by Father Rick Frechette, MD. With no marketing—since any budget goes towards treating those Haitians who cannot afford medical treatment—Saint Damien Hospital's work has been highlighted worldwide through the visits of several Influencers such as Susan Sarandon, Demi Moore, and Mario Bello. None of these visits have been paid for by Saint Damien. Instead, Influencers have been added to various existing trips, usually facilitated by third-party organizations in response to a natural disaster, such as the devastating 2010 earthquake.

Auction Items or Donations

Asking an Influencer for an auction item or experience is perfectly acceptable. For a Multi-Pact between Morgan Stanley and the Grammy Music Education Coalition, an auction via

Charity Buzz, Influencer donations included a guitar lesson with Jack Black, a coaching session with producer Louis Bell (Camillo Cabello and Post Malone), and a meet and greet with Mark Anthony.

I'd recommend that money not be on your list of requests. Visibility and connection to your desired audience are worth more than a donation. However, on several occasions, without being asked, I have worked with Influencers who made an unpublicized donation to an organization they visited or a cause they supported.

Around the Ask

Delivery Method

Your Influencer may be on set, at a training camp, in their bedroom making TikTok videos, or chilling on vacation. Asks made by email are the way to go since they can immediately be forwarded to your Influencer. Snail mail, while a novelty, is ineffective for an Ask due to the longer time scale, the difficulty forwarding, and the chance of your letter being lost.

Volume of Asks

Whether you Ask one Influencer or many at a time depends on the Ask. If it's a social media post, going out simultaneously to many Influencers is perfectly acceptable. For an Ask with a higher degree of Influencer involvement, such as a voice-over, keynote, or gala honoree, it's best to prioritize and make your request one person at a time. While not ideal, sometimes you need a Tier One spokesperson and don't have the luxury of waiting for, say, a couple of weeks for your first choice to say yes or no. Here you make the Ask to numerous Influencers, and if two or more say yes, you may have a problem, but it's a good problem to have, and you will likely always be able to work with both on your campaign.

> **Pro Tip:** I find that going out to twenty Influencers and their teams, and then doing the same for a second batch of twenty a few days later, and so on, makes the process more manageable and less arduous.

Timing

Pick your moment. Please don't make an Ask to an actor when they are filming a hit show or to a basketball player in the middle of the playoffs, and expect them to be available, or even respond, straight away. To get Daymond John of *Shark Tank* fame to visit Year Up's program at West Los Angeles College, I needed almost six months of patient persistence since he was filming. But when it happened, the pay-off was memorable for the students, Year Up, and Daymond. You can usually find out online who is doing what, when, and where, and if not, the Influencer or their team will let you know their availability.

Payment

A few philanthropic organizations pay their Influencers. Bristol Palin, daughter of former vice-presidential candidate Sarah Palin, was paid $262,500 in 2009 by the Candie's Foundation for taking part in a campaign to warn against the consequences of teen pregnancy.[32] I know of several other examples that are not public. Paying, to me, lowers the public's trust and reduces the Influencer's effectiveness.

I don't generally pay Influencers. You don't need to pay, either. I have worked on cause campaigns with many of the world's best-known celebrities, including queens, archbishops, virtuosos, MVPs, Academy and Grammy Award winners, and none of them got paid. They volunteered their services because we matched the cause and their passion through effective research. What I do is avoid agents. Their role is to ask for money. Instead, go to Influencers directly or through their other representatives, such as their manager, PR agent, lawyer, or personal assistant. They look at these requests through another lens, with an eye for opportunities that will elevate their client's public profile, make them happy, and do good. I also clarify that this is a philanthropic cause, and the Influencer was chosen because of their alignment, which implies no payment is on offer. Rare exceptions to the no-payment rule is paying a small honorarium to the Influencer's charity of choice in lieu of a fee or a very reduced fee to a social media influencer.

---

32. Rosen, "Sex Abstinence Work."

There is a digital divide between a so-called celebrity and a social media influencer. The former's ecosystem is more mature and encourages celebrities to support charitable causes. In contrast, the latter is a younger system that hasn't yet embraced philanthropy in the same way. Social media influencers get paid for social posts, which are their primary source of income. Unfortunately, many social media influencer platforms and managers are relatively new and understandably profit-oriented. So while some will offer their client's services at a nonprofit rate or even for free, most do not. It's not offensive for them to ask for money because you are asking them to do their job for free, and while not ideal, it's important to keep their perspective in mind. As I work with more and more social media influencers, I try to educate them and their teams, and as this world matures, I believe that philanthropy will increasingly play a more significant role. For ALIMA, an international medical relief organization, various micro Influencers from the medical community posted for free or for a fraction of their regular fee, and in certain cases posted several times for the one price.

While Influencers in the main do not get paid for promoting philanthropic causes, they do for commercial campaigns. These fees can range from several thousand to millions of dollars. The variables that determine price are the brand, the Influencer, the length of the campaign, and what they are asked to do.

- In between philanthropic and commercial campaigns sits cause marketing, where a company has a philanthropic initiative that also promotes their brand or product. For cause marketing, especially if a Multi-Pact is created, the costs are significantly less than you'd pay for a commercial campaign.

• The corporate partner's costs are regular marketing costs such as creative and ad-buys, although these costs are typically significantly lower than a traditional marketing campaign.

• For the Influencer, I'd say their participation cost is zero to twenty-five percent of their usual commercial fee.

• For the nonprofit, they receive a donation or a financial guarantee. The guarantee is usually that the campaign will raise not less than $X for the nonprofit partner. So if the public doesn't donate 100 percent of the dollar goal, then the corporate partner makes up the difference. This may be more cost-effective for the company than making a donation.

Taco Bell's 2011 cause marketing campaign—itself a Multi-Pact—asked its customers to donate $1 to their "Graduate to Go" initiative over a two-week period. The money went for teen graduation programs, and in return, the customer got a taco voucher. Influencer Mark Wahlberg appeared in TV spots and in a media campaign promoting the cause, and in return, his Mark Wahlberg Youth Foundation received $450,000 towards its work with inner-city youth programs. This payment was a fraction of what it would have cost for Mark to appear in a Taco Bell commercial, assuming he would have at all, and the campaign generated goodwill with the public, its employees, and franchise owners.

> **Pro Tip:** *You will still need to pay reasonable pre-approved travel, accommodation, and related expenses for a philanthropic, commercial, or Multi-Pact campaign. These costs will generally be higher for commercial campaigns but, in all cases, need to be monitored so as not to mount up.*

Approvals

Allow time for key stakeholders, colleagues, or partners to approve or review your Ask letter. Over the years, I have learned that having another set of eyes on the Ask letter is helpful. Your independent reader may spot an error or make a suggestion that improves your Ask. It also vests them in the process. When asking for approval, please give a drop-dead date for a response.

Who Do You Ask?

A well-crafted request letter is worthless unless the right person reads it. Get it to that right person, and your chances of a yes increase dramatically. Influencers have a cadre of people to support them. Usually, an actor or musician has three or four, and an athlete or businessperson one or two. Your best contacts in priority order are the Influencer; the Influencer's personal assistant, manager, PR or communications professional; the head of their foundation; other associated staff;

friends and family; the Influencer's lawyer, and their agent. Here is how to approach these folk.

The Influencer

Having a direct conversation with an Influencer is the holy grail. The Influencer hears about the campaign firsthand and sees how passionate you are about it. If you are fortunate to be in this position, be cautious, don't overwhelm the Influencer, and certainly don't insert yourself into a conversation the Influencer is having with someone else. Sometimes the Influencer will say, "yes, that sounds exciting," and you go away full of hope, only to have their management later reject your Ask. The reason is that you have caught them unaware, and they are always getting hit up when in a public setting. My suggestion is to have a conversation and request the best contact info where you can send follow-up information. This way, the Influencer's team is not undermined—a sure way to get a no—and they can review your Ask with the Influencer later on.

Managers

Managers look after the Influencer's overall career. Many managers, personally and on behalf of their clients, genuinely believe in the power of the Influencer Effect to create positive change. I continue to work with a plethora of managers who have the best interest of their clients at heart and want to do good. These enlightened managers are responsive and engaged and often have a designated person on their team who handles philanthropy and social justice for their clients. In the music space, I particularly enjoy working with John Legend and Lindsey Stirling's manager, Ty Stiklorius, whose Friends At Work management company has philanthropy and social justice at its core. Many others, including Roc Nation, SB Projects, and Red Light Management, have dedicated in-house philanthropy staff. Those managers who are not so hands-on will pass your request onto the Influencer's PR agency.

Public Relations & Communication Professionals

PR executives have a difficult job and an unjust reputation as blockers rather than facilitators. They constantly protect their Influencer's public persona by finding the best media opportunities at the optimal moment and rejecting requests that are not in their client's best interests. Generally, I have found communication professionals to be helpful, although they can be overwhelmed, so you may need to follow up a few times to get on their radar.

Foundation Heads

Several Influencers have their own foundations to focus on a particular cause they want to impact. An Ask to their foundation's executive director may get you a quicker response than going through management. Recently I moderated a panel on music and mental health for the Rotary Clubs of Los Angeles. Maya, the executive director of Lady Gaga's foundation, Born This Way, was a valuable participant. Often the Influencer's philanthropic team is more in tune with and more sympathetic to social causes. I continue to advise, or support pro bono, several Influencers and their foundations on their philanthropy (but alas, not Born This Way).

When I am on the receiving end of a request, I look out for what is best for the Influencer. Does the Ask and the campaign fit their interests, risk profile, and schedule? A significant other factor is, "Will the campaign have measurable impact?" However, whatever my recommendation, the final decision is always the Influencer's and their team.

Associated Staff

Many athletes, especially those that play on a team, can best be reached via their team's communications, community, or marketing department. Exceptions include high-profile players such as LeBron James, Ronda Rousey, Lindsey Vonn, John Cena, and Roger Federer, who each have their own personal reps.

Approaching an Influencer through their reps also applies to other teams or ensembles such as dance companies. Misty Copeland may have an agent, but staff at her dance company, American Ballet Theater, would be my first choice to contact.

Friends and Family

Most Influencers grew up in regular families, and still hang out with—or put in positions of responsibility—friends from their youth. If you know an Influencer's friend or family member and are close enough to ask them to make the Ask for you, do so. Brad Pitt was an ambassador choice for the Rotary "End Polio Now" campaign, and it turned out that a Rotarian knew his brother, also a Rotarian, and made the Ask. While Rotary is a large organization, local connections or a small Rolodex can build effective partnerships. Just make sure you simultaneously make the Ask officially to their team, so nobody's nose is put out of joint.

Lawyers

Entertainment lawyers are part of and a conduit to the Influencer's team. They will pass on a request to the Influencer or their team. Finding out who reps which Influencer can be tricky, but a search reveals a lot. For example, the top two search results on Google for Lady Gaga's attorney turned up her litigator, Orin Snyder, and her transactional lawyer, Allen

Grubman. These search results are correct since I know Orin through my music networks, and Allen Grubman was Jive Records' external counsel. I could also confirm the search results' accuracy by going to Orin's page at his law firm and seeing that his list of clients includes Lady Gaga. Allen's law firm doesn't have a page for individual lawyers, but I found plenty of references to Allen representing Lady Gaga. Lawyers are not the final decision-makers but usually get you to the correct member of the Influencer's team.

Agents

For a brand undertaking a commercial campaign, sending the Ask to an Influencer's agent is the right way to go. However, if you are a nonprofit or a cause marketing campaign, ask an agent only as a last resort. Agents are not interested if there are no dollar signs attached. That's their job, even if they are sympathetic to your cause.

> **PRO TIP:** *You can go to a speakers bureau to hire an Influencer for a speaking engagement. There are many reputable ones like the venerable Washington Speakers Bureau. But beware, as certain speakers bureaus purport to represent an Influencer when they do not. I'd suggest using a speakers bureau only if you have budget. Otherwise as a research tool to identify specific Influencers that are attractive to your target audiences.*

How to Find Contact Information

Finding the contact information for a particular Influencer's representatives can be tougher than researching the Influencer. Say I originally chose sixty Influencers, ultimately rejected twenty, and decided to go out to forty. It would have been a waste of time and resources to research all original sixty contacts. Search for Influencer's contacts only when you have finalized and prioritized your outreach list.

Check contact details each time you do outreach, since Influencers frequently change PR agencies, managers, and other reps. You may write to a particular rep, thinking that they are the contact, and they will tell you, "I no longer represent this Influencer, and so-and-so now represents them." If you have a contact but are unsure of its accuracy, make a phone call to confirm it. Otherwise, you waste or delay all the excellent work you have done so far. Most reps will let you know if your contact is up to date.

Below are some tips for how to reach out to Influencers.

Aggregator Platforms

Mega and some macro Influencers generate enough money to support a team of representatives such as managers, agents, and PR. However, most micro and nano Influencers do not. This lack of representation can make it harder to contact them, but in recent years, many platforms have grown to aggregate Influencers, making it easy for brands to contact them. Specific platforms, like Captiv8 and CreatorIQ, offer a one-stop-shop approach by aggregating millions of Influencers. Others specialize in a particular sector, like Neufluence that works with BIPOC and LGBTQIA+ Influencers, and has both a platform and bespoke service. A brand with a specific campaign reaches out to one of these platforms and chooses several Influencers it wants to engage. The platform will also suggest other Influencers and will negotiate a fee on behalf of either the brand, Influencer, or both.

Direct Message

Another way to connect to an Influencer, especially a social media influencer, is to direct message (or DM) them via their website or social media platform, such as Instagram. Influencers' social media sites are run mainly by their social media managers, who will pass on the messages to their team. Certain Influencers do read their followers' DMs and occasionally respond. Several have been motivated to act following a DM request from a fan, such as going on a prom date (Shaun White) or paying college tuition (Nicki Minaj). While these Asks paid off, your odds of success are way longer. You are most likely to get a response to a DM if you ask the best way to contact the Influencer and why you want to do so. Usually, if the Influencer is interested, you get back a contact email address to make your Ask.

Free Influencer Contact Services

Over the years, I have looked at numerous free sites that purport to give you contacts for Influencers' reps, but none have been reliable, complete, or up to date enough for me to recommend them. The better ones (relatively) give out addresses, not emails. The chances of snail mail ending up in the right hands and being given consideration in a timely fashion are minuscule. Other sites that allegedly provide you with celebrity phone numbers and show text exchanges with Influencers feel inauthentic and are designed to sell you something. Stay well away from them. Overall, I actively want to dissuade you from using these free contact services.

> **Pro Tip:** For local Influencers such as on-air talent, a call into their station may elicit a response. I did a random test with local Memphis TV station W-REG and sent an email using their "Contact Us" form, asking if I could book on-air talent for a local charity event through them. They responded.

Paid Contact Services

There are various contact services that charge one-off, monthly, or annual fees for access to their database. Several of these are reasonably accurate but expensive, while others are unreliable.

Below are both the inexpensive and costly options. Other tools, if worthwhile, are reviewed on the book's website, goodinfluencebook.com.

- **Hunter.io:** This email finder software gives you a limited number of free email address or verification searches, and then you pay around $50 per month for the service. If you know the Influencer or their representative's domain, and it's in the email address you found, you know that the email address is likely correct.
- **IMDB Pro:** There is a free version of IMDB, but IMDB Pro has contact information for people and companies associated with movies, documentaries, TV shows, and video games. Search results provide details of the cast members and how to get in touch with each of them. As many athletes and musicians often appear in these kinds of productions, you will find their contacts here as well. The accuracy of contact details across categories is pretty good, and at $13 per month, it's inexpensive.
- **Captiv8:** A powerful tool that does much more than gathering contacts, Captiv8 is an expensive option for this purpose. Captiv8 is an Influencer analytics platform and marketplace that uses artificial intelligence to connect brands with relevant Influencers. The platform shows Influencers' demographics on who follows them in real-time, and helps brands identify which audiences the Influencers attract. I have used it for several months and find it helpful for my research and outreach. The downside? Contact details tend to be telephone numbers, not

emails. At $12K or more a year, you need to be a brand, a sizable nonprofit, or in the Influencer business to afford it.

With diligence, you will find a point of connection to the vast majority of Influencers. However, certain specific Influencers are just difficult to reach. Bill Murray does not have an agent or any publicly available contact information. For the Rotary polio campaign, we reached out to his sister Nancy, a nun and polio survivor. If you have persistence, you will find a way, but unless a specific Influencer is the only one for you, weigh the effort-to-reward ratio, and find another suitable candidate.

Who Makes the Ask?

Answering the question of who the best person is to make the Ask is not always simple. The Ask can come from your organization directly, an ally, or an outside vendor. Each has its advantages.

Organization

If you are a well-known brand such as Mercedes, Pepsi, or WeChat, or the nonprofit equivalent such as the Red Cross, Oxfam, or UNICEF, then an Ask coming directly from you will carry significant weight. Organizations of this size regularly employ a staffer dedicated to talent relationships.

In reality, any organization, irrespective of size, can succeed in making an Ask to almost any Influencer on the planet directly or via an agency. Entertain Impact has been around for nearly two decades and has a good reputation throughout the industry. When my agency makes an Ask, the Influencer or their team knows that the client has been vetted, the cause will resonate, and the campaign will be professionally handled.

Close Ally

On occasions, a client will say that they, a friend, or a contact has a relationship with one of their identified Influencers, and would I mind if that person also reaches out with an Ask. While I have made many contacts and friends over the years through my entertainment and social impact work, I do not know everyone. If anyone supportive of your campaign offers to reinforce an Ask, gladly say, "Yes, thanks." They may have a closer relationship or have known the Influencer longer. Perhaps they went to the same school, are family friends, or grew up together. These secondary Asks from credible sources reinforce yours and help get Influencers onboard. Just ensure that you oversee the timing, follow-up, and outreach of each Ask so the process is efficient and well managed.

Outside Vendor

Certain agencies specialize in booking talent for commercial events and charge a fee with a minimum to get talent to appear. The total cost can add up to several thousands of dollars for a nonprofit and hundreds of thousands for commercial brand campaigns. For this fee, your representative will wrangle the talent, make the introduction, and ensure the paperwork is in order. The rest is usually up to you to handle. This category comprises giant agencies or communication companies, and at the opposite end of the spectrum, several personal boutique firms or individuals. Many have been around for a while and are reputable, others not so. Please do your homework before paying any fees.

I do not do one-off Asks, such as an appearance at a gala. I turn down these jobs. My interest is in a deep, long-term relationship with my clients through campaign work that facilitates their mission and yields positive social change. I suggest you do these one-off Asks yourself or go to an individual talent relations specialist or talent wrangler as they are known in the business to do so for you. Their sole focus is to get an Influencer for you. They will not create or execute your marketing or advocacy campaign. Usually, wranglers come out of the entertainment business, where they specialized in talent relations. You pay a fee, usually five to ten percent of what you are paying the Influencer, with a minimum price for a commercial job and a set fee for nonprofit outreach. However, these fees are negotiable. My suggestion would be to make the one off Ask yourself initially or try to foster a long-term rather than a one-off relationship.

Entertain Impact makes the Ask at least 95 percent of the time. Still, on occasions, I will, at my cost, engage a third-party vendor who has better connections in, say, a particular area such as hockey, a specific country such as Kenya, or knows a particular Influencer well. There are several talent relations specialists that I have developed trust and rapport with over the years, such as Angela Fisher of AMF Entertainment, who has supported Entertain Impact's client's campaigns.

After the Ask: Keys to Success

You've hit "send." Now what? Sit back and wait? Nope. There are a few more things you need to do to improve your chances of success.

Tracking System

You may make dozens of Asks during each campaign, so a method of tracking them helps you be on top of your outreach and reduces any administrative burden. An Excel spreadsheet or Google sheet is a simple but effective form of tracking grid.

I use these categories to track Influencer outreach for each campaign:

- Name of the Influencer and their contact and details
- Outreach undertaken (yes/no)
- Ask: if the Asks are different, I highlight the priority (e.g., social media post versus event attendance)
- Follow-Ups (yes/no and dates)
- Response (yes, no, or maybe)
- Next Steps

PRO TIP: *Have two tabs. One is for the Influencers that are still in play, while the other tab is for those who have said no.*

TOP TOOLS

A more sophisticated approach to tracking your outreach is to use a software program. There are several around. I like Pipedrive, which is relatively simple to learn. Once you do, you have a handy tool not just for your Influencer outreach but also for your business development generally. Pipedrive is a customer relationship management tool that automatically tracks and then organizes the calls, emails, and other actions you have taken to get a customer. I especially like the visual aspect of the program, where you can create your headers. You could make each of the columns I stated above in Pipedrive and track outreach. If you do loads of outreach, Pipedrive may be for you, but if you are undertaking one or two outreach efforts a year, stick to Excel.

Follow Up & Timing

Let's assume you have made your Ask and are waiting with anticipation for a reply. A week passes, and no response. You follow up for several weeks via emails and calls, getting more and more anxious, and start to worry you will miss your campaign deadline. This process may be frustrating, but realize your Ask is one of many that an Influencer's team has to deal with each day. If you are disappointed or affronted by the lack of a response, it is not personal or a judgment on the validity of your cause or campaign. For every campaign, a substantial portion of your outreach may be no-responses, even if you have the correct contact information. Other types of responses are discussed in the next section.

Outreach is not about sending an email, sitting back, and doing nothing more. The amount of emails we all get is overwhelming. How many times has a person sent you a follow-up email reminding you about their original email that has been lost in your inbox? While persistence is a necessary quality in outreach, people are busy and under stress, especially in the time of COVID, so be empathetic to those on the other side of your request. Kindness goes a long way.

I have found this follow up system works:

Day 1: Original Ask sent.
Day 8: Gentle follow-up.

Day 15: Call to ensure they got the Ask. When calling, simply say that you are following up on your email, explain the Ask in two sentences, and see if they want you to resend the email.

Day 20: Follow up with the date of your event or deadline.

Day 28: Send a thank you. Whether they said no, or even if you haven't heard back and you have decided to move on, send a thank you. You may want to work with the Influencer or their team in the future.

Response Types

Responses to your Ask come in four categories: yes, no, silence, and maybe.

The most obvious one is a YES. Celebrate. We will talk about how to move forward on this basis in the next chapter.

The other obvious one is a NO: disappointing to hear and will be a large proportion of the responses you will get. Analyze your noes since there are different types. There is the, "No, we're not interested," and the, "No, we're too busy, but re-approach us again in a few months." The latter is far more encouraging and results from establishing a connection between your campaign and the Influencer. Where I am cautious is when I get an immediate no. This means either the Influencer has a set list of acceptable topics for engagement, and requests pertaining to any other are an automatic no, or the request never got to the Influencer. Here you need to make a judgment call. If you feel your request was ignored, ask a second time politely by email explaining the applicability of your Ask to the Influencer. This follow-up often results in it being given proper consideration.

Silence is tricky because you make assumptions about possible motivations or responses when you don't hear from your Influencer. The lack of a response could be because you used the wrong email address or that circumstances in their private life don't allow them to focus on the request. So my rule is that if I haven't heard back anything after three follow-ups, I treat it as a pass. This way, I can move on and not have a lingering uncertainty that can be time-consuming and stressful.

A maybe is an in-between response and leaves you hanging for several weeks while the clock runs down. This limbo situation is uncomfortable. You are torn between the hope that you will get a positive answer and the need to move on. My suggestion is to set a drop-dead date by which you need to hear back. Put this date either in your original Ask letter or in your follow-up email. This deadline concentrates the mind and allows you to turn a maybe into a no or yes.

When dealing with the Influencer's gatekeepers, remember that a rep's day is intense and hectic. Like you, they are juggling many opportunities for their Influencer who may be on a remote island doing a shoot, out on tour, or on a well-deserved "do not disturb" family vacation. While they may want to support your request, their turnaround time may not be as quick as you would like. This lack of communication can make you feel exasperated, but temper your desire to say something nasty, even if you are near your launch date. Delete what I call your therapy email—you know, the blunt, angry one you wrote that may ruin the relationship forever. Then take a deep breath and go to a meditation class or work out. Please never express your negative feelings to the Influencer's team. Basically, the simpler you can make their lives, the better your chances of success. Professionalism is paramount.

Closing the Deal

If you got a YES, you will need to memorialize the understanding between your organization and the Influencer. A phone call will not suffice. Use one of these three ways; all may be morally binding, but some are more legally binding than others.

Email

An email simply states the basic terms and is sufficient in most cases where it's a nonprofit campaign or no money is changing hands.

Memorandum of Understanding (MOU)

The MOU sets out the essential and practical deal points and is used when money changes hands and there is not enough time to sign a full-blown contract.

Contract

A contract is a formal document detailing each party's rights, obligations, and remedies. Usually used for brand campaigns when payments are involved, or for larger organizations like Pepsi or UNICEF. The main terms of a contract are as set out below, but you can take the ones you want and put them in your email or MOU:

- **Practical terms:** Names of parties, description of the campaign, what the Influencer is responsible for doing, what you are doing, when, where, what times and dates, approvals and turnaround times, and payment and expenses
- **Legal terms:** Warranties, indemnification, notices, choice of legal jurisdiction, confidentiality, and signatures

Samples of each are on our website, but as I am not a practicing attorney, you will need legal advice prior to entering into any agreement.

Next Steps

Once you have made the Ask, be prepared for when an Influencer says, "I'm in." When I Ask(ed) John Legend for a quote for inclusion in the press release for the campaign to preserve Nina Simone's childhood home, the quote was pre-approved by the African American Cultural Heritage Action Fund. So when John's management confirmed his participation, the quote and press release went straight to John and his team, who kept the basic sentiment of the quote but adapted it to John's voice.

Engaging Influencers can be a frustrating and rewarding experience. Frustrating because you go out to many Influencers, wait for what seems like forever, and continually get rejected or, worse still, don't even hear back. And rewarding because inevitably, your hard work will pay off, and you will get a "Yes, I'll support your campaign." Then you will feel exhilarated and be able to move forward to the Activation phase. That is the tip of the iceberg, the part the public engages with. It is essential that you execute this Activation phase well, so let's see how to do just that.

CHAPTER 5
STEP 4: ACTIVATE

Well I'm gonna quit talking and take action now
—Elton John, "Texan Love Song"

Congratulations. You got a YES. All those hours of strategizing, research, and outreach have paid off. Enjoy the euphoria—for a moment—then, take a deep breath and get straight back to business. The world will never know all the hard work that brought you to this point; all the public will see is each public-facing marketing element of your campaign, known as an "Activation," such as a fun run, gala, or Instagram post.

Possibilities abound for Activations. They come in all shapes and sizes and are only limited by your imagination and resources. That stated, all the campaigns I work on these days are either solely social media focused or have a substantial social media component. Relatively, social media is an easier lift than other forms of Influencer Activations since you and the Influencer can respectively create and participate in this type of campaign without leaving the comfort of your office or home. Unlike traditional media, it also allows you to address the public with no intermediary. Other advantages are that social media Activations have little or no associated cost, take less time, and preserve bandwidth compared to other Activations. By contrast, traditional media is expensive and limited. In 2012, *The New York Times*'s daily circulation was nearly two million; today, it is under a quarter of that. Yet a full-page advertisement in the US Edition can run upwards of $100,000

Hopefully, in your Action Plan, you diligently set out your social media strategy, calendar, and selected your platforms. If not, now is a good time to do so.

> **Pro Tip:** *If your campaign relies solely on the power of Influencers, you will do yourself a disservice. You still need strong concepts, messaging, and content.*

If you are tempted to skip social media for your Activation, first consider this: with social distancing during the COVID-19 pandemic, there were no live concerts or theater performances, and no TV or film production going on, so Influencers had time on their hands and were eager to help. You couldn't get on Instagram, TikTok, Facebook, or YouTube without an Influencer asking you to stay home, praising the essential frontline workers, or raising money for the multitude of causes that needed public support. In-home concerts and DJs spinning from their living room became people's distractions. D-Nice, a former Jive artist, had over 160,000 people in one night at his Instagram Club Quarantine "Homeschoolin" event, with the live chat feature used by many famous folks: Drake, Oprah, Will Smith, and Michelle Obama amongst them. Social media is your direct connection to your audience, and Influencers the conduit.

Activations with Influencers other than social media range from the simple to the complex. A visit I arranged for Isabella Boylston, principal dancer extraordinaire for the prestigious American Ballet Theater to the National Dance Institute in Harlem was as simple as a couple of calls and a subway ride. More involved, although I was not, was Isabella's work as a brand ambassador for the Calzedonia "Create Your Own Stage" campaign. Isabella shot a video dancing to a backdrop of iconic New York landmarks while modeling Calzedonia tights. Also, Isabella undertook press resulting in articles in *People*, *Domino*, and various industry publications.

An Activation that launched in May 2022 was the release of an album *Bangsokol—A Requiem for Cambodia* by the composer Sophy Him, commissioned by Cambodia Living Arts on my label, Entertain Impact Records. Apart from containing beautiful and emotional music, the album is a means to honor the dead of the Cambodian genocide and a vehicle to talk about the role of art as a healing mechanism in a post-conflict society. To support the album's release, I planned various Activations, including an Influencer campaign, a PR push, a panel, and the creation of multiple assets such as a promotional video, re-mixes, and a Non-Fungible Token. This Activation required a team, expertise, and funding, which I built up over decades in the music business and at Entertain Impact. Most other Activations require far less effort and work. For example, a keynote, a gala honoree, a panel, and an auction item are all potential Influencer Activations that almost any organization can pull off well.

The number one reason Activations fail is poor execution. If well-executed, you can have measurable success. If not, you will waste a significant opportunity to benefit from the Influencer Effect. After over one-hundred campaigns, I have found some best practices and workarounds that make Activations effective, whether you're engaging an Influencer for commercial gain or philanthropic purposes. While not meant to be a panacea, you'll find many valuable stories, suggestions, and insider tips in this chapter to make your Influencer Activations successful.

There are three stages of any Activation: before, during, and after. For simplicity, and because an Activation is like a movie or TV show, I like to call these stages pre-production, production, and post-production. Get each one of these stages right, and not only will you reduce stress levels, staff time, and costs; most importantly, you'll have the impact you want.

Pre-Production—Setting Up for Success

Activations come in many shapes and sizes. Whether a TikTok influencer is promoting your product or a local news weather person is hosting your fundraiser, you need to plan to succeed. Your Action Plan, created in Step 1, gives you a broad campaign framework. Having researched and successfully engaged your Influencers in Steps 2 and 3, now you'll need to make a detailed plan for each specific Activation.

The more preparation you put in, the better your outcomes. When I was head of Business and Legal Affairs at Jive Records in 1986, I met a teenager named Will Smith. He was one half of the newly signed Jive act Jazzy Jeff and the Fresh Prince, and now he's an international movie star. How did he achieve that status? Modestly, Will has said, "I've always considered myself to be just average talent, and what I have is a ridiculous, insane obsessiveness for practice and preparation." The incident at the 2022 Oscars with Will show the pressure that celebrities are under, and while Will reacted inappropriately to a cruel joke, I believe he will learn, assess, and reemerge in a better place. One take away from this is the country spent more time on this than talking about the Ukraine war or climate change. This, to me, further demonstrates our fascination with Influencers.

The time you spend on pre-production is time well spent. Give yourself the longest possible lead time you can. Start planning months ahead of your Activation since time tends to run quicker than anticipated. Every minute you devote to pre-production can save you many hours putting out fires at the production stage. Of course, the time you spend on pre-production will vary depending on the level of complexity of the Activation you're planning. For the first of four, half-hour filmed interviews I did with various Influencers for Promundo's "Global Boyhood Initiative" campaign, the planning time between logistics, interview questions, locations, tech, client input, producer meetings, and talent outreach was over four hours. I needed just one hour of planning for each of the other three interviews once we had our system in place. My advice is to make a conservative estimate of the time you think you will need and double it. If you don't use the time, you get it back.

Pre-production has several essential components. Some (like budgets and calendars) are concrete, while others (like content creation or relationship management) are less tangible. To handle each part, it helps if you are both left- and right-brained. If not, allocate tasks according to your own and your colleagues' strengths. Let's start with goals and the practical stuff.

Goals

During the "Design Your Action Plan" stage earlier in the book, you set S.M.A.R.T. overall goals for your campaign. Activations need to be ideated and prioritized through the filter of your campaign objectives.

When you have several parties involved with a campaign, such as with a Multi-Pact, however well-meaning, their goals will not always be the same. If you are the corporate partner, you will likely want to promote your brand, engage employees, strengthen customer loyalty, connect with your desired audiences, increase sales, and do good. While grateful for the corporate support, the nonprofit partner's goals are to raise money, awareness, and support to further their cause. Much like your goals, the Influencer will also have their goals; primarily to make a difference and, secondarily, to ensure their image is protected. Typically, companies, nonprofits, and Influencers come together around mutual goals for an effective public-facing Multi-Pact campaign. That doesn't mean all their goals must be the same, but they need to be aligned and not in conflict with each other. Reconciling goals is usually done through discussion, good faith, and compromise, especially in a Multi-Pact. Once alignment exists, then the Influencer Effect will kick in, and each participant wins big.

Singer, songwriter, and producer Pharrell surprised NYC middle school kids in the middle of them performing his hit "Happy" and two of his songs from the then-upcoming movie *Hidden Figures*. Afterward, Pharrell talked to the media about the importance of universal music education and his new movie. This marketing partnership between music nonprofit A.M.P. Up, Fox 2000 Studios, and Pharrell hit each party's goals. The Activation drove traffic to the movie, promoted Pharrell's music, and put pressure on education departments for improved music teaching in public schools. Each party in this Multi-Pact benefited far more by partnering than undertaking solo Activations.

> **Pro Tip:** *Ensure everyone's goals, including your own, are clear, communicated, and agreed upon before your Activation.*

The Practical Stuff

Budget

You created an overall campaign budget in your Action Plan, with an estimated cost for Influencer and other Activations. Since completing that budget, you've refined your concept and strategy, identified Influencers, and know what specific Activations you will be doing. Now it is time to review and, if needed, adjust your overall campaign budget and create a sub-budget for each specific Activation.

A word of caution: The tendency most people have when creating an Activation budget is over-optimism. This means people allocate too little money to individual Activations and therefore exceed their budgets. That's not good for you or your organization.

> **Pro Tip:** *When budgeting, be realistic about the costs. Add a 10 percent contingency. If you have not spent the contingency after the Activation, that's a bonus.*

When constructing your budget, don't be cent-wise and dollar-foolish. Entertain Impact once paid $300 for a car service to pick up an Influencer for a site visit. Why? On the day before the Activation, my nonprofit client decided that it was not in their budget, even though they had agreed to pay for transportation. Reneging was shortsighted since the visit generated over $10,000 of earned media coverage.

Set aside time and do your research when putting together your final budget. The less time you dedicate to these tasks, and the later you leave it, the more your costs will increase. Lock-in contracts early to save money. If you wait to hire a photographer three days before an event, you will pay above the market rate, and your choice of available photographers will be limited.

Be disciplined when managing an Influencer Activation. Stick to the budget you set, but be practical if unforeseen circumstances arise. That's why you include a 10 percent contingency into your overall budget.

Vendors

In your business operations, you likely use vendors regularly for repeatable services such as accounting, technology, and insurance. When it comes to Activations, it's less likely that you regularly engage with the specialty vendors you might need, such as a production company, make-up artist, or event planner. If hiring for services you are unfamiliar with or outside your comfort zone, do your research and remember that three quotes and references are a must. On several occasions, I have nixed a vendor based on poor references. Conversely, I have found many of my favorites through referrals. This way, you can get a sense of market rates and conditions. With each conversation, you will get to hear new, creative ideas and benefit from the vendor's experience as it applies to your Activation.

When you land on your vendor of choice, please do not merely accept their fee quote. Negotiate. If your Activation is cause-related or philanthropic, a vendor may be willing to give you a reduced nonprofit rate or throw in additional services, such as providing lighting for a photoshoot at no charge. If you don't ask, you don't get.

Once you have made your vendor choice, be sure to memorialize in writing the agreed-upon terms. Include a detailed breakdown of the services or goods to be provided, the deliverables you will receive, and other essential terms such as the cost, location, and timing. This way, you won't get a surprise at the end of the job with a bigger bill than you expected. If you're a nonprofit organization, keep in mind that most vendors, me included, go well above and beyond the call of duty when working with cause-driven organizations. I estimate that my agency delivers over $3 in services for every $1 paid by a client.

> **Pro Tip:** *Over time, build up a database of your go-to vendors for future use.*

Sponsors

Sponsors are often the lifeblood of Activations. Companies sponsor cause-related events either through their marketing department or their foundation. There are many creative ways to get your sponsor's name in front of your target audience, such as adding it to your step and repeat (red carpet photo backdrop), jersey, or by serving their exclusive drink at your event.

Sponsorships and how to get them are an important subject area, but I won't go into much depth in this book. However, what is written here about Influencers can apply to your sponsor. Books like *The Sponsorship Seekers Tool Kit* by Reid and Grey, and companies like For Momentum, are good resources.

If you have secured sponsors for your Activation, please make sure that you have everything in place ahead of the big day so you can fulfill your part of the bargain. You may have agreed to provide your sponsor with prominent signage at your event or to include them in a press release announcing the Activation. Have those elements prepared and get your sponsor's approval in advance.

Information Sheets

What time does the event start? What time will the car pick up your Influencer? How long is the keynote? Prepare information sheets well ahead of time, so everyone will know what to do, and your Activation will run smoothly. I won't say I like dealing with details, but Activations are successful because you take care of them. The information sheets aggregate all necessary information. Here are the main ones you'll need:

Production schedule

An Activation can occur over more than one day. The Influencer may need to make a two-day trip to speak at your conference, plan for a four-day international field visit, or even a three-week series shoot. This document sets out in detail everything that happens and who is responsible from pre-production through post-production of an Activation. Items covered include the name, date, and type of Activation, each stage, dates, hotels, transportation, flights, who is accountable and how to contact them. It's a mini version of your campaign work plan.

Call sheet

A call sheet shows what is happening on the day of the Activation. It is an industry term for a one-pager listing of what will happen, with who, where, at what time, and lists each person's contact details, titles, responsibilities, and transportation. Note that you should always use the contact details for your Influencer's personal assistant, manager, or PR rep, and never the Influencer's contact details unless you have explicit permission.

Run of show

A run of show is a guide for the creative team and the clients, detailing exactly how an event will unfold from start to finish. You can use the run of show for any Activation. I recently produced *Bravery Is*, an IGTV series featuring artists like Kevin Bacon, Justin Michael Williams, Ziggy Marley, and Chelsie Hill. They spoke about raising boys and shared their art on the subject, and the run of show looked, in part, like this:

- Introductory footage and title card
- Interviewer makes the introduction, 30 seconds
- Interview: Ziggy and interviewer, 5 mins
- Music "True To Myself" plays, 3 minutes
- End title cards

Run of shows are also used for live events. When constructing one, don't schedule too tightly. Build in time for late arrivals, people chatting to your Influencer, and other unforeseen holdups. When I was working on the Master of Ceremony portion of the Bill and Melinda Gates Foundation's Global Vaccine Conference in Abu Dhabi, Bill Gates was scheduled literally down to the second. However, theory and practice never coincided. Bill always ran over. As with your budget, you need a 10 percent time contingency.

Specific details included on these information sheets may need to be reviewed and agreed upon by your

Influencer well before the Activation. In particular, agree on the choice of transportation, food, and the start time.

> **Pro Tip:** *At the Activation, have several paper print-outs of the contact list and run of show to hand out to the Influencer and their team.*

Transportation

Whatever the occasion, when an Influencer needs to arrive somewhere, there is always the worry, even if unjustified, that they will be a no-show. You can remove this anxiety by coordinating the day, time, and nature of transportation. Will they be using a car service, or will they drive themselves? If a plane ticket is involved, what class will they fly?

> **Pro Tip:** *Standard operating procedure is always to send a car rather than have an Influencer drive themselves. It allows the Influencer and you to relax and to know they will turn up on time.*

You will need transportation available throughout the duration of the Activation. You never know precisely when an Activation will end, and you need to be prepared to transport your Influencer back home. Also, if something unexpected occurs, such as someone leaving their speech at home, having a car at your disposal is a must. While this can be expensive, you don't need to hire a stretch limo. Negotiate an all-in deal, called a wait and return, or have a responsible and insured volunteer available to drive.

Accommodation

Because most Activations last only a few hours, accommodation is usually unnecessary. In the few cases where your Influencer needs to stay overnight, determine in advance the hotel class, and type and number of rooms required. It's customary to cover the costs for the Influencer plus one additional person for an event or trip. The plus one may be a personal assistant, friend, or partner.

Where big costs can kick in is on international trips. For example, when *The Good Wife* actor Archie Panjabi went from the United States to India as an ambassador for Rotary's polio eradication campaign, the costs could have been over $40,000, including travel and production costs. However, Archie's manager, Raj, worked with me in advance to reduce the international airfares and hotel fees to under half of the original budget. The publicity earned from Archie's hospital visit in India and elsewhere had value many times in excess of the cost. It also re-energized Rotary's membership and deepened the relationship between Archie and Rotary. This relationship resulted in Archie keynoting the annual Rotary convention, appearing in public service announcements, and being the emcee for the Gates Foundation's Global Vaccine Summit in Abu Dhabi, which raised $4 billion—75 percent of the projected budget at the time—to achieve a polio-free world.

> **Pro Tip:** *Be firm and say no if, on the odd occasion, the Influencer's agent Asks for an entourage to travel. There may be exceptions, such as when an A-lister needs a personal assistant and security, but generally, it's an unnecessary cost.*

Food

The old saying that a well-fed crew is a happy crew is a maxim used in film and TV production, and for a good reason. If your Influencer appears in a shoot that lasts several hours, having good quality food available for them, their team, and your crew is the norm and expectation. Budget time for craft services to set this up, or for your intern to do a food run, and for the Influencer and crew to eat. Be sure to allocate money to cover this expense.

Aside from courtesy, food helps your Influencer maintain their energy level and creates a positive atmosphere. I worked on the social impact campaign for *Love & Mercy*, a movie about Beach Boys' Brian Wilson. Brian is a gentle, unassuming man, and during a recording session with middle schoolers to promote music in schools with the nonprofit Little Kids Rock, he asked for his favorite order from In-N-Out Burger.

Appetite satiated, Brian played on for another thirty minutes, giving our director his best take of the day.

> **Pro Tip:** *Find out in advance about any dietary restrictions or preferences, and provide a compatible menu. In your run of show, be sure to allocate time to eat. If you are keeping your Influencer at an Activation long enough that you need to provide a meal, unless it is a gala, photo, or video shoot, take a step back to consider whether you are asking too much of your Influencer.*

Dress Code

If the Influencer is attending your gala, they'll need to know if the dress code is black tie, white tie, creative black tie, black-tie optional, business casual, cocktail, festive, smart casual, fancy-dress, or themed. Let them know with enough time to get the attire they need. Whatever the event, sending a one-liner on dress code helps avoid your Influencer turning up in a full-length ball gown when everyone else is wearing jeans.

Year Up is a nonprofit that provides intensive job training, internships, and support for underserved high school graduates ages 18 to 24 to help them launch their careers. When I accompanied *Shark Tank* star Daymond John to visit Year Up's Los Angeles program, Daymond wore casual clothes, but the students were dressed in business attire. I had forgotten to let him know the dress code. Daymond is an exceptional public speaker, and he captivated and motivated the young people, and frankly, nobody noticed. However, I did, and it never happened again.

Social Media

When your Activation includes asking your Influencer to post to social media, your job is to draft the post and ensure that the Influencer's team approves the content. Send your messaging, visual content, and tracking code to the Influencer's team two or more weeks in advance. This way, they can review, approve, and schedule the post. Ask your Influencer to post on a specific day, usually the day of your campaign launch, and I recommend a second post a short time later. Remember, yours is not the only post: most Influencer teams make numerous posts per day and keep a running social media calendar. Be polite but be persistent in getting the post approved. Your Influencer's team is busy, so don't feel bad about following up with them. This way, you are on their radar screen.

> **PRO TIP:** *The earlier you get content to the Influencer team, the better your chances of getting the content you desire posted on the day you want.*

Image

One of the most sensitive areas for an Influencer is their image or public persona. Before any Activation, determine and agree whether photos and video will be taken. If the answer is yes, ask your Influencer to be camera-ready when they arrive or provide hair, make-up, and styling beforehand.

When the public is involved, even for a casual appearance such as at a hospital, Influencers know that everyone has a smartphone, and photos will be taken and posted on social media. In other cases, such as a photo shoot for a brand campaign, your Influencer might need hair, make-up, and styling, although, in my experience, this requirement happens less and less as a natural, makeup-less look is currently in vogue.

Providing these services can be expensive, as Influencers often have their preferred hair, make-up, and stylist people. Expect to pay a couple thousand dollars a day for each. If the cost of the Influencer's people is out of your price range and the Influencer agrees, have your production company recommend alternatives.

COVID-19 and Zoom have made our Influencers much less concerned about keeping up appearances. Hopefully, this trend continues post-pandemic. However, for every action, there is an opposite reaction, and I suspect there will be a glam wave after the COVID-19 pandemic lockdowns have relaxed.

> **PRO TIP:** *Rather than buying clothes for your Influencer's shoot, have the stylist use their connections to borrow a dress from a fashion house that can be returned after the shoot. This standard operating procedure helps keep costs down, and in return, the brand gets free publicity.*

Talent Release Form

Most individual Activations do not require a contract. A simple email setting out the terms and expectations is acceptable. What you will need, however, is a talent release form. The release is a one-page legal document that the Influencer or their rep signs allowing you to use their image, performance, bio, and services for your specific purpose, e.g., a photo for a campaign.

An Influencer's PR rep will ask that you give the Influencer approval rights to their image, photos, and press release. On occasions, they may limit your use of these image rights to a set time period, such as two years. This restriction stops you from using the Influencer's photos years later, making their client look dated and potentially damaging their image. Agree with both conditions since they are standard gives.

Many Influencers simply sign the talent release form on the day of the Activation. Take a copy of the talent release with you, and don't be afraid to ask for a signature at the Activation. Make sure your release covers everything you need. You will find a sample talent release on the website, but please note, I am not giving legal advice, and you should consult a lawyer.

> **PRO TIP:** *When you are paying an Influencer for their services, you will need a contract. In those cases, a simple email containing expectations and a signed talent release form is insufficient. Be sure to consult your attorney. For nonprofit or cause-related Activations, I discourage paying your Influencer as it severely reduces the value of their involvement.*

Clearances

If you are using music or a photo that you didn't commission, you'll need to get permission or clearance from the rights holder. The adage of "you can use eight bars of music or a photo you found on the internet for free" is, to put it politely, incorrect. As I write, fitness company Peloton is being sued for upwards of $150 million by numerous music publishers for using their music in exercise videos without consent.

Clearance requires that:

You know that you need to clear the content

My rule is that if in doubt about whether you need to clear the content, clear it or don't use it. You could face a potential legal claim of several hundred thousand dollars plus legal fees. Sony Music generously provided wonderful photos of Nina Simone for the African American Cultural Heritage Action Funds' campaign to preserve Nina's childhood home. I advised the Fund not to use these photos to promote the campaign since that would have constituted an advertising use for which we needed consent. As the photographer was long dead, and tracking down his relatives in the time available was problematic, the photos were given away to donors who pledged more than a certain dollar amount.

Please, don't take the chance, assuming you won't be caught using images without permission. Creative Photographers Inc.—Pam my sister-in-law and my brother Geoff's agency—represents a number of the world's most successful photographers. A percentage of their agency's revenue comes from settlements for unauthorized use of photos. Amazingly, among repeat offenders are many of the world's largest companies, all of whom should know better.

> You know the owner of or who
> controls the rights to the content

Finding out who owns or controls the piece of content you want to use is not always an easy thing. Nowadays, Google Images has made it easier to track down a photo, but it is trickier to track down the owner of music's two components—the recording and the composition. In many cases, a song has multiple composers in addition to the performer. For example, "My Way," recorded by Frank Sinatra, The Sex Pistols, and Elvis, was originally a French song, "Comme d'Habitude," with lyrics by both Paul Anka and Thibaut Giles, and music by Claude Francois and Jacques Revaud. There are two publishers, Chrysalis and Concord, who control the composition, and if you used Frank Sinatra's version, you would also need to contact Capital Records/Sony Legacy, who owns the recording.

As this example illustrates, when you want to use music, you must identify all the creators and find the rights holders that represent them. This process is challenging, even with access to databases such as All Music, ASCAP, and BMI repertoire searches. I have needed to call a senior executive at a music company to get music cleared numerous times. You likely won't have that same luxury, so avoid popular songs, where possible.

> **PRO TIP:** *Go to a company specializing in pre-recorded, pre-cleared music for licensing, such as Heavy Hitters Music or Associated Production Music. You can search the music online, get creative guidance from a music director, purchase a low-cost, all-in-one license for the composition and master combined, and download the recording on the spot—all in under an hour.*

Allow enough time to get the clearance

Rights owners have limited resources to clear their intellectual property, and like Influencers, get many requests. These companies are typically understaffed and overworked. By necessity, they prioritize requests. If they have to choose between, say, clearing a song for a movie—such as 2016's animated *Sing*—for a fee of several hundred thousand dollars, or your request for a gratis use, guess who will get priority? After many months your request may rise to the top of the low priority pile, and even then, allow more time as the rights holder will, in most cases, need to go back to its client—the creator—to get their sign off to your use.

Using again the example of the song "My Way," after you've taken the time to find the owner or the entity who controls the rights, the rights holder would likely need to contact the composer and artist for their permission to allow your requested use. Sony Legacy, for example, would need to go back to Frank Sinatra's estate to get their consent for the "My Way" use, taking even more time. It is a very frustrating and archaic process.

The one exception to the above advice would be cases where the artist is directly and deeply involved with your cause. Contact the artist's manager, and if management approves your use, their publishers and record company usually fall in line.

Negotiating terms, signing the agreement, and paying the fee

While I always ask for a free license from the rights holder, and many grant this request, I will, when needed, offer a small fee, say $250, to cover their administrative costs to cut down on the time it takes. Certain rights holders will offer a nonprofit rate, but you can negotiate or choose something else if you feel you are getting charged too much. Otherwise, you pay the money, sign the paperwork, and off you go.

Clearances are needed but are painful. Where possible, use content you or an engaged Influencer controls.

Publicity Plan

Get your publicity plan and team in place ahead of your Activation. Your first critical decision is whether you will take on publicity yourself or bring in an outside PR agency. Make this decision way ahead of the Activation, because the moment it's over, you'll need to reach out to the media, and not waste precious time researching, briefing, or engaging an agency. There are pros and cons to both options. Money and the size of the market you want to reach are two.

If you are a local organization, say for example a store or food bank in Kansas City with few resources and a local (versus national) presence, do publicity outreach yourself. Make a list of the local radio stations, newspapers, and blogs, then find a contact for each. Walk in or email your press release, photos, and a brief memo. Follow up with a phone call. Write the story for the media. Local newsrooms have limited resources and will be more receptive if you make their job easier.

However, if you have a decent budget and a national footprint, consider spending the money on a PR or communications agency. Each agency has its market focus, and within one agency, each individual will have their specialty.

O'Dwyers, which ranks PR agencies by industry and city, is an excellent place to start when selecting an agency.

However, a personal recommendation—not just for a particular agency but for a specific person within an agency—is the best way to go. Ask around. People in your circle, or friends of theirs, will know. Fees for a six-month contract (which many PR firms insist on as a minimum) range from $1,500 to upward of $15,000 per month, plus expenses. There may be lower nonprofit rates or pro bono services available if you ask.

Of course, the big agencies tend to be more costly, so I have found that a successful formula is to hire a former partner from a major agency who has gone solo or started a small agency. For example, I worked with Jean Sievers, whose client Jeff Bridges participated in Share Our Strength's "No Kid Hungry" campaign. An excellent PR professional with decades of relationships with the media, Jean knows who to call, and most importantly, people pick up when she does! These individual practitioners have experience, excellent contacts, and lower overheads, making their rates more reasonable.

If you plan on doing most of the outreach yourself, you can share the press release, video, and photos via one of the major PR distribution services such as PR Wire, PR Web, and Cision. These services will push out your material to thousands of news organizations, social channels, and websites, who then have the option to pick up the information to use in a story. You can also monitor and analyze how you did through these outlets. Costs start at under two hundred dollars and go as high as several thousand dollars, depending on the service or segment of the media market you choose.

The Creative Stuff

Now, let's turn to the creative side of Activations.

Creativity Counts

Creativity really does count. It is often overlooked and under-estimated, but it is as important to get right as the practical stuff. Throughout my music career, I have heard many financial investors ask questions about revenues, expenses, and operations. They never ask about the one critical factor for success in the music business: How good are your ears? Meaning: Creatively, how good are you at identifying and nurturing talent? As expert as someone may be at the business side, they will fail unless they have hit records to generate revenue. To find the next Ariana Grande, Billie Eilish, or Drake is a rare talent in its own right.

While you may not be pursuing a music business career, your successful Influencer Activation requires creativity in order for it to have longevity and impact. Just contrast these two campaigns' creative elements: (1) three Air Force Assistance Fund's PSAs have been seen by less than six thousand people on YouTube over a five-year period despite the beneficial work the organization undertakes, or (2) WeAreAmerica's eponymous PSA featuring John Cena, where the Influencer Effect garnered over thirty-six million views in a far shorter period. While the Influencer Effect certainly played a large part in disparate viewership, the creative look and feel of the different videos played a significant role in their watchability.

Ideas

If you want to get ideas for creative campaigns, check out marketing awards such as the Cannes Lions or the Webby Awards. A campaign I was deeply involved with was honored by the Shorty Social Good Awards, which acknowledge "the most effective and creative use of social media by a nonprofit." I worked on the philanthropic part of a Multi-Pact combining Usher, State Farm, and the Chattanooga public schools. Called the "Neighborhood Sessions" campaign, components included a concert and TV show in Usher's hometown of Chattanooga. The award-winning campaign provided music resources and teachers for third graders in twenty elementary schools that previously had none. An unexpected consequence was that parents of children in other grades in the school system wanted the same for their kids, and the enlightened school district hired nine more full-time art teachers. The Shorty and other awards have many commercial and philanthropic categories, and you can in good conscience get inspiration from those campaigns that are nominated.

Content Creation

On many occasions, I see businesses and nonprofits succeed in enlisting an A-lister's services only to produce weak
content that has no impact or longevity. With 24-hour news
cycles, a tsunami of information crashing over everyone,
and low attention spans, the more creative the content, the
better your chance of cutting through the clutter. You don't
have to spend a fortune, but you need to produce excellent
marketing materials to a professional standard. Hiring the
right producer, camera person, designer, or event planner is
vital to creating good content. This way, your desired audiences will take notice.

Content creation can be one of the higher ticket items
in your budget—by thinking creatively, you will cut down
costs. One way of doing this is to piggyback on an existing
production involving your Influencer. I was engaged by the
movie studio Participant Media to undertake the social impact
campaign for the movie *Breathe*. The lead actors in the film—
Claire Foy and Andrew Garfield—were busy on other projects,
so they had limited availability. Additionally, arranging for
them or our crew to travel to shoot material for our campaign
would have been costly. Fortunately, *Breathe* was opening the
Toronto film festival, and both actors would be in town on the
promotional junket. The studio's publicity team agreed that
the actors could shoot a public service announcement (PSA) on
polio eradication for us while doing their promotional interviews in Toronto. The script was written with our nonprofit

partner Rotary's input and approved by the actors and the studio PR teams two weeks before the shoot. There was no cost, the whole shoot took fifteen minutes, and the PSA was broadcast-quality. Taking advantage of these opportunities will produce better marketing materials at lower costs.

A powerful, creative project has additional benefits on top of how it will affect the outcome of your campaign. Influencers, especially actors, musicians, and social media personalities, are very image conscious. If your marketing materials are outstanding, not only will they be highly competitive in a crowded marketplace, but Influencers will want to work with you again. If good enough, the campaign could also qualify for recognition from the Platinum PR News Awards and the Shorty Awards, both of which have honored philanthropic campaigns I have produced in nonprofit and commercial categories. These accolades further your brand and organization's reputation. So be creative.

Your Audience is What Counts

When you are creating content, put yourself in the headspace of your intended audience. What may seem like a great idea to you may not resonate with the people you want to attract the most. So if your campaign gets lots of media attention but upsets people, that negatively impacts your brand.

Take Pepsi's tone-deaf "Live for Now" Super Bowl commercial featuring model Kendall Jenner, who leaves a photoshoot to join a passing protest with a Pepsi in hand. The worst moment is when she gives a police officer her Pepsi, causing protesters to stop and applaud. The commercial created such an uproar for trivializing Black Lives Matter that it was yanked from the air within 48 hours. It was apparent that Pepsi had failed to vet the commercial with its intended audiences sufficiently.

Pepsi spent and lost millions, and their blunder highlighted the company's lack of diversity in decision-making, leading to nine months of the lowest perception rate in eight years for the brand. Worse still, millennials' consideration of purchasing a Pepsi plummeted to its lowest level in years. A tearful Kendall apologized via social media and addressed the controversy on her reality TV show. One additional point: Kendall, a top-ten social media influencer, had no history of serious activism and would not have been the ideal choice in the first place for this type of advert.

Speeches, Talks, and Keynotes

If you ask your Influencer to speak, whether it be a few appreciative words at a fundraiser, testifying before Congress, or as the keynote at your national conference, you'll want them to be comfortable and informed on the subject. To have your Influencer spokesperson be uneducated on your brand, cause, or organization is embarrassing to all concerned. A few weeks before the Activation, send a few talking points, along with a brief memo—a paragraph or two—on your organization and the Activation. Make sure you bring a paper copy of the information on your organization, and any talking points, remarks, or speeches with you to the Activation itself as a backup in case your Influencer forgets their copy.

Most Influencers are professional and will have read the information beforehand, but it's best practice to have a backup to offer in case not.

> **Pro Tip:** *Don't surprise your Influencer by asking them to make a few impromptu remarks in front of a crowd without asking them ahead of time. The golden rule applies here. Don't do it to them if you wouldn't want it done to you.*

When an Influencer is going to be giving a speech, I will often write the first draft and give it to the Influencer's team. This draft allows you to control the narrative, ensuring that the Influencer conveys the information you want. It also makes life easier for the Influencer. Most will appreciate this and will adapt the content to their style.

Many Influencers testify on behalf of a charity before Congress and state and local government committees. In this environment, you have no control over the questions officials will ask, nor how the Influencer will respond. The vast majority of Influencers you work with will have been involved in that specific cause for many years and are already well-educated and effective at speaking in these contexts. For those Influencers who are just starting on their philanthropic journey, they may be passionate but not experts on your cause, so try to avoid using them for this specific purpose. Of course, if you must do so, proceed only with dollops of caution and much preparation.

Take late-night TV's Stephen Colbert, who appeared before Congress in 2002 on behalf of the United Farm Workers of America as his conservative talk show host character. There had been a segment of his show in which he worked for one day picking beans and packing corn at a farm in upstate New York. His oral testimony departed drastically from his written statement and was comedic in nature. While amusing and serving to raise awareness in the media, he didn't get the right messaging across, and a Republican congressperson walked out of the hearing. Stephen, who usually does terrific things for philanthropy through his AmeriCone Dream Fund, did not move the issue forward with Congress.

Contrast this with his predecessor on late-night TV, Jon Stewart, who gave emotional testimony on behalf of the 9/11 first responders in support of restoring their medical benefits. Jon has fought tirelessly for first responders and military veterans for decades, and sits on the 9/11 Memorial Museum board. On his TV show, John has supported the passing and reauthorization of the Zadroga Act to provide medical monitoring and financial aid to 9/11 responders. Jon is an excellent example of how, with an engaged Influencer, all you need to do is convey your goals for the hearing, suggest supporting arguments, and let them take it from there. That's what happened when the authentic and informed Jon Stewart testified before Congress. Media coverage was ubiquitous, the public was outraged, and the Zadroga Act was permanently reauthorized.

Conference keynotes are an ample opportunity to engage an Influencer. Having an Influencer introduce a panel, perform, or talk for a few minutes is very worthwhile. A word of caution: these are usually much less satisfying in the doing than in the envisaging. Audiences are attracted by a name but often feel unsatisfied by the Influencer's speech. Be careful not to alienate both the Influencer and your key stakeholders by selecting an Influencer who doesn't have an authentic connection to the topic.

Influencer Relationships

Let's turn to what is often the most difficult area for us all: the nebulous world of relationships. How you deal with the Influencer and their team is vital to whether the Activation happens, is successful, and forms the basis for a potential long-term affiliation. Who is the right point person in your organization to manage these critical relationships with your Influencer and their team? The point person guides them through the Activation and interacts with them the most.

Irrespective of your organization's size, you are best served if your contact point with the Influencer or their team is relatively senior, mature, flexible, respectful (not reverential), and can get things done internally. Communications or marketing experience is a significant positive in the role, as is having a calm, professional, and personable attitude.

The point person is usually the CEO or executive director for smaller organizations. Larger organizations typically have a senior staffer with communications experience or a dedicated talent relations staffer.

You have multiple important external relationships in your organization, such as the board, shareholders, major donors, vendors, volunteers, and customers. Like these folks, Influencers dedicate their time, equity, and brand to your cause. Your whole organization should treat Influencers and their team with the same high level of professionalism and respect as you would any other meaningful relationship. Be responsive and always follow through. Here are some of my key tips for interacting with Influencers and their teams, and what to keep in mind in order to have the most successful outcome possible.

Respect the Gate Keepers

Managers, PR professionals, or personal assistants are the gate-keepers whose job is to protect and promote their Influencer clients. Deal with them in a professional, timely, and efficient manner. These reps are, in general, good people who want to support cause-related endeavors. If they feel your organization is good to work with, they will encourage the relationship, and much goodwill will come out of their support. However, if you are disorganized or present a risk to their client's reputation, they will end their client's involvement with you in a heartbeat.

Keep the Long View in Mind

I cannot stress enough how meaningful it is to have strong, mutually beneficial relationships with your Influencer and their team members. They truly matter. You'll need to manage and nurture your relationships with the Influencer and their team and always take a long-term view. My relationships from over thirty years in the music and film business have led to positive results for Influencers and nonprofits that I could never have imagined. Will Smith was nineteen when we met. Three decades later, after little contact, I on behalf of the Music and Youth Development Alliance reconnected via the Will and Jada Smith Family Foundation on its campaign for under-resourced youth on career paths in the entertainment industry. No one can predict the future or where we will end up in life, but if you like, respect, and treat people fairly, the law of karma kicks in.

Know the Dangers of Reneging

Reneging is the nuclear option of Influencer engagement. What you absolutely cannot do is ask an Influencer to be involved, and then after the Influencer says yes, withdraw the offer or significantly renegotiate the terms. Reneging on your agreements will destroy your reputation and your relationship with your Influencer and their reps.

Several years ago, I offered to pay for a keynote speaker's flights and hotel expenses when a nonprofit client reneged on paying these due to exceeding their budget in other organizational areas. This nonprofit had an annual budget of over $20 million per year but was disorganized and had an incompetent senior staff member who replaced the executive who had originally brought me in. In the end, after a forthright conversation with the senior staffer, the nonprofit decided to cover the costs, and the Influencer went to the conference blissfully unaware of the behind-the-scenes machinations. However, after other warning signs, this was the final straw, and I fired this client. Later, I found out that I was not the only one who'd had difficult experiences, including prior agencies and staff members who'd left in droves. As I aim to do good, and new leadership had just come in, I gave a pro bono report with suggestions for improvement. While I never got an official reply, the incompetent senior staffer no longer works there and the organization is in a much better position to deal with Influencer engagement.

Now that you have done your prep work, the question is, "Will it be all right on the night?"

Production—It Will Be Alright on the Night

By putting in the work upfront, you have gone a long way toward creating the conditions for a successful Activation. Now, the big day has arrived, and you need to execute well.

If the basics aren't covered—the car is late to pick up your Influencer, for example—it doesn't matter how nicely you apologize. You're off to the worst possible start, and your organization looks amateurish. On the other hand, if the car arrives on time and at the correct address, no one is going to mention it, and you are off to a good start.

Staffing

Your Activation needs the proper staffing to run smoothly. Below are the most essential staff you need, excluding third-party vendors you may need to hire, such as a production or catering company:

Gofer

You will always need bodies for the mundane and unexpected tasks that can and will occur such as your Influencer forgot their speech, or needs an In-N-Out burger. A gofer is a person who runs errands for you. They "go for" this, that, or the other, hence the name. Your gofer can be a staff member, an intern, or volunteer, so long as they are low key, courteous, and together. You need a gofer so you can stay focused on the big picture.

Chaperone

The chaperone is a person who guides the Influencer and their team at the Activation to ensure that everything goes smoothly. They meet the Influencer as their car arrives, chaperones them, and is responsive to their—and their team's—needs. If anyone on your team has experience with talent, that is the best person to be in this position. Otherwise, an adult who will not act like a fan can serve in the role of chaperone. A chaperone provides a certain comfort level to the Influencer, as they know they are being taken care of. It also sends a message to their team that they can rely on your organization to take care of business.

Communications

A comms staffer who can work with the Influencer's PR team is a real value-add. Your staffer can get releases signed, work on social media posts or the social live stream, and get any approvals needed, e.g., for remarks, photos, and the press release. If you don't have an internal person or can't afford an outside agency, divide these tasks between your chaperone and leadership representative.

Leadership

Your Influencer will want to meet the head of your organization, usually your CEO or executive director, or for a larger
company or nonprofit, the chief marketing officer. Adding the
right board member into the mix is never a bad thing. Having
important people from your organization spending time with
your Influencer is a good way to show them that you value
their efforts. It is also an opportunity for the Influencer to
learn directly from leadership about your work, which can
deepen their connection to your organization.

> **PRO TIP:** *Prepare a briefing memo on your Influencer
> for your leadership so they know your Influencer's story.*

Attitude

Your team is the public face of your organization. Please
brief them that they need to be respectful and professional.
Remind them that knowing an Influencer's character on TV
or having read about them in the media is very different
than knowing the Influencer in real life, and absolutely is
not the same thing as being their best friend. You don't want
anyone on your staff to be a fawning superfan who ends up
with a restraining order. Treat the Influencer as if they were
an executive or board member. That said, sure, you can ask

for a photo with your Influencer at the end of the Activation, since being famous is part of their job description.

No Extras

Another no-no is pushing the Influencer to do things on the spot that were not part of the original Ask. This intrusion makes the Influencer very uncomfortable, feel exploited, and, despite their connection to your organization's mission, can cause them to withdraw from any future involvement.

> **Pro Tip:** *On-set etiquette is crucial. If an Influencer appears in a video for your campaign, they are working in an environment where they are an expert. By all means, be present and nearby, and certainly be friendly, but leave your Influencer alone to focus on the work at hand.*

Prepare for the Live Audience

You may have public events as part of your Influencer's media appearances, such as an instore, live stream, or town hall, where the Influencer takes questions from a live audience. Control this as much as possible. Vet and select the questions before you go live. This way, you can make sure you and your Influencer are comfortable answering them.

> **Pro Tip:** *With Zoom, you can use the private chat function to message your Influencer during the interview without anyone else seeing it. If it doesn't confuse them, this means you can feed talking points or facts during the interview. Just be sure not to interrupt the flow of the interview.*

Cost Overruns

Inevitably, there will be a surprise on the night that leads to additional costs. Your Influencer runs late, and the crew goes into overtime, you want the photographer to shoot more than you agreed, or the weather does not cooperate, and you need a tent! Decisions that have cost implications need to be made on the spot. Anoint one person with authority to make these calls with an agreed-upon budget limit. For example, give them the power to spend up to 10 percent more in each category with an overall cap of $3,500. This way, calm and order prevail.

Life Gets in the Way

On infrequent occasions, after spending months planning your campaign and preparing all the materials, an unforeseen event occurs at the moment of launch. For example, your Influencer gets food poisoning the day of your product launch. In the business, the technical term for this is, "Sh*t happens." On rare occasions, a tragedy occurs that is so serious that it takes up all the media's attention.

I launched a campaign for World Animal Protection on

the day of the worst mass shooting in US history. 58 people were murdered, and over 850 people were injured at the Route 91 Harvest Music Festival. Out of respect for the dead and injured, no Influencers—nor I—wanted to move forward with the "Wildlife Selfie Code," which involved posting selfies with sloths. The campaign didn't meet its goals, and I refunded part of my fee. When something heinous like this happens, please don't get angry at its impact on your campaign. Learn from it and, where possible, share the lessons.

Now that the Activation is over, your next and final task is to get the word out to the world.

Post-Production—Be Loud, Be Proud, and Be Heard

To adapt an old Zen proverb, if an Activation happens, but no one knows about it, did it really happen? The answer is an unambiguous no. You need to get the word out to your targeted media and audiences as quickly as possible. Even a day's delay makes your Activation yesterday's news. If you're efficient in releasing your story, your cause or brand will attract awareness, support, and money.

Social Media

Social media is not static; it's interactive. This interaction between you and other social media users is part of community engagement, where your aim is for others to see your content and follow you. Build up your list of Influencers, donors, partners, and other users that you follow, and engage with them regularly. Community engagement can be time consuming, but once an Influencer has posted and endorsed your campaign, it's crucial that you engage in a timely fashion with that Influencer's post. You want to make sure to say in a personal, not generic way, "thank you," and like, retweet, share, comment, or do whatever is appropriate. Apart from acknowledging your Influencer, more people will see the original post.

Distribution

Content needs to reach your desired audience, and the platform you choose to use will depend on the audiences you are looking to attract. As discussed earlier in these pages, the rule is to go where your audience is by using the appropriate platform with specific content created for them.

Image Approvals

You wouldn't want your name, photo, or quote to be released to the public without your permission. For the most part, nobody does. Companies and nonprofits have approval channels, as do Influencers, whose image and public persona are critical to their brand. You need to get approvals before sending anything to the media about your Influencer. Note image approvals derives from—but is separate to—a talent release form.

You don't need a signed approval letter—an email will suffice. Compile all the content you want to have approved—press release, photos—and a short description of your uses for each item. Send this to a rep, who will likely reply with questions, request changes, impose a condition, or sometimes simply with approval. Occasionally, a representative will approve with conditions; the most common is a time limit on use.

Failure to get approvals promptly will delay your marketing and promotion, which is a huge opportunity lost for your cause. Old news is no news, so your Influencer Activation is far less potent the more time passes.

> **PRO TIP:** *Have your press release and any existing photos agreed on before the Activation. This way, you are ready to go out immediately after the Activation. If the photos or videos were taken at an event, try and get approvals within an hour of the event ending and the photos distributed to media shortly thereafter.*

Appreciation

When you do something for someone, you appreciate receiving a thank you. The same applies to your Influencer, who just donated their time and reputation to your cause. A handwritten card or letter from the executive director or a senior company staffer, accompanied by a small gift, can mean so much to an Influencer.

Be creative with your gift. I gave Daymond John of *Shark Tank* a box of shark-shaped chocolates, and Celine Dion got a 1938 dime pendant from March of Dimes, being the year the organization was founded. Those musical artists that appeared on an album for Rotary's polio eradication campaign each received an album plaque. A small but meaningful gesture will have a favorable effect on your future relationship with your Influencers.

Lasting Relationships

Your aim is for your Influencer to feel that participating in your Activation was time well spent, made a difference, and was put together by a professional organization. This aim applies whether your Influencer is a local athlete or an Oscar-winning actor. If you had a successful Activation with your Influencer of choice, where everything went smoothly and your Influencer and their team enjoyed their experience, follow up to make sure this was not a one-and-done.

You have an opportunity to engage your Influencer in a long-term relationship with your brand or organization. Depending on who the Influencer is and their availability, you can make a subsequent Ask. If the Influencer is very engaged, your Ask could be for shooting a video for your organization, appearing on air to talk about your mission, or making a public visit with a local elected official. Ideally, do this shortly after your Activation, so the event is still top of mind for them.

Kevin Bacon and his brother Michael were the first celebrities I engaged with when I started Entertain Impact. Even though I didn't know them, they kindly hosted my VH1 program *Between the Covers* for free to support an album to raise money for the then-named T. J. Martell Foundation for Leukemia, Cancer, and AIDS Research. I have had a relationship with the Bacon brothers ever since, which over the years has led to several philanthropic Activations and my working with Kevin and his SixDegrees.org foundation on various causes, ranging from cancer research to youth development and hunger. Our long-standing relationship means both Kevin and Stacy, SixDegrees.org's executive director, feel comfortable working with me and the nonprofits I suggest to them.

Influencer-led Activations that work well are things of beauty. When you have completed yours, take a moment to breathe and celebrate your success. You got the media coverage you wanted, built a relationship with your Influencers, and reached new audiences. Now comes the big question: Did your campaign make a difference?

CHAPTER 6
STEP 5: MEASURE

We measure success by how many people successful.
—The Carters, "Boss"

You did it! Your campaign launched. The buzz, the media, and the jubilation are all intoxicating. But did you make a difference? Did you move the needle? Are the subjects of your efforts better off, worse off, or in the same place?

For me, one of the most exciting and frustrating parts of my work is measuring a campaign's success. Early in my career, I just wanted to do the work, and I didn't realize the importance of measuring outcomes. By the time I understood how important it was to measure results, I never had the in-house expertise or wasn't able, for a reasonable price, to hire experts that went beyond pretty dashboards or word clouds. I also found that often clients couldn't provide me with the necessary information since they had not bought into the need to measure as a way of strengthening their organization. These days, I have measurement in a much better, albeit not perfect, place.

Why We Measure

Entertain Impact exists to make a difference in the world, so I measure to seek the truth. Not everyone feels the same way. These are the main stumbling blocks that I have come across that prevent people from implementing measurement protocols:

- Lack of confidence: People are afraid that they will lose face or standing within their organization if campaign goals are not met. So they shy away from looking at the facts.
- Lack of knowledge: Senior management doesn't feel it is important, so people within their organization simply don't have the training or tools to do it.
- Lack of resources: I hear, "we don't have the time, people, or money to dedicate to measurement." So no resources are dedicated to measurement.

I understand each of these hurdles to an extent, but you can't learn, improve, or succeed if you don't measure. You'll also know quicker if a campaign component is not working or money is being wasted. No one needs to set up a measurement and evaluation department to measure effectively but most departments such as accounting or human resources do measure. And you will benefit internally and externally by doing so. The information needed is often readily available and is easy and free or inexpensive to collect. You can pay as little as $49 per month for a media monitoring tool, and many of Google's suite of tools such as analytics, surveys, and news are free.

Focusing on, and making people accountable for, measurement will make measurement part of your DNA and lead to improved results. In other words, you become what you measure. For example, if you decide you want to measure customer acquisition, you will inevitably focus on that aspect of your campaign, and become more effective at customer acquisition.

Collecting, analyzing, and evaluating the available data allows you to see where you came from, where you currently are, and where you are going in the future. Specifically, it will enable you to:

- show the results of your efforts with a particular campaign and tie these back to your goals
- identify, reflect, and pivot during an existing campaign
- gain proof and support for future campaigns
- see how you compare against your competitors
- adjust and improve your measurement capabilities
- learn what works and does not, the risks involved, and implement new approaches going forward

For Usher's "Nancy Lackey Arts Education Fund" initiative to increase the number of art and music classes offered in Chattanooga's elementary schools, the campaign hired Dr.

Marclyn Porter, an evaluation expert, to measure agreed-upon metrics over three school years. Metrics included the number of additional schools and students who received these classes following the start of the campaign. Measurement showed that the elementary schools with art and music education for third graders increased by more than 60 percent, and approximately 1,500 students received this essential learning. Social-emotional learning, academic success, or community health was not measured due to a lack of funding. However, quantitative or anecdotal evidence of other impacts came from students, parents, and teachers. Especially gratifying was discovering that non-English speaking immigrant parents from Central America were joining their kids at Saturday morning school arts events. This activity was their only contact with the school since they were uncomfortable attending parent-teacher conferences or other official events. By measuring, we could see that Usher's campaign made a difference in the lives of Chattanooga's elementary students and their families. The next step for this campaign is to take these results and approach businesses and others in the community to get additional funding to introduce art and music classes to more schools and expand summer programs.

There is also a moral element to measurement. It's important to ask yourself, "What is the likely effect that the act of measuring, or the information uncovered, will have on my subjects, stakeholders, and campaign?" Often the simple act of observing changes reality. The observer effect shows that by observing a situation or phenomena, you disturb and change it. In quantum physics, light can be a wave or a particle depending on if it's being observed or not. Digital marketers use algorithms and cookies to track our behavior and serve up adverts that play into our interests, searches, or word uses. This raises the question whether a consumer genuinely wanted to buy a product or donate to a cause or was persuaded to do so as a result of being observed and then, depending on your perspective, manipulated or helped. In your work with people, your act of tracking and measuring can affect the situation (have you ever altered your behavior because you knew you were being watched?), so be mindful of your actions and their potential consequences.

Over the years, measurement has proven that most of my clients' campaigns have made positive contributions. By showing your campaigns do the same, you will have the opportunity to generate support for yourself, your future projects, and your organization.

Who Cares What We Measure?

Knowing who you are measuring for will inform what and how you choose to measure. On the one hand, you are your most important audience: you measure to improve your own results during current and subsequent campaigns. But almost as important are your stakeholders. We know that stakeholders are those people, groups, or entities interested in, or involved with your organization, or who can affect or be affected by your or your organization's actions. Your organization, campaign, or other initiatives need their support to be successful. Let's look at each member of a Multi-Pact and the main stakeholders of each. When you are deciding which metrics to track during a campaign, you'll want to think about which stakeholders you want or need to inform about outcomes. This will depend in part on your campaign goals.

Choosing Your Audience for Measurement: Stakeholders to Consider

	Multi-Pact Member		
Stakeholders	**Company**	**Nonprofit**	**Influencer**
Board Members		✓	
Shareholders	✓		
Investors / Funders	✓	✓	
Donors		✓	
Senior Management / Management	✓	✓	✓
Employees	✓	✓	✓
Customers / Clients	✓	✓	
Fans			✓
Social Media Followers	✓	✓	✓
Family			✓
Community	✓	✓	✓
Industry	✓	✓	✓
Vendors	✓	✓	✓
Media	✓	✓	✓
Analysts	✓	✓	
Policymakers	✓	✓	

The audience for your campaign metrics will vary depending on each stakeholder's role or may vary depending on the type of campaign. Just ensure you consider what information these stakeholders will want to see when you determine what you want to measure.

When We Measure

When you created your Action Plan, you set goals for your campaign. Before you start measuring, review your goals, determine what insights you want to get from the data you acquire, and how you will implement improvements based on lessons learned. In your Action Plan, you will have established how to collect the data you want to measure. Your advanced planning will make reporting your campaign results so much easier because some types of metrics will be unavailable once the campaign starts unless you establish the tracking tools and calculate your baselines ahead of time. Even collecting the most rudimentary metrics are so much better than doing nothing, and you get the measurement muscle working by simply getting started. Measurement allows you to identify and reap the rewards of your labor.

Measurement is, by nature, a comparison between at least two things, whether you're looking at two different times (beginning and ending), organizations, (your peers or competition), or data points (users and control group) compared at the same time.

Establishing a baseline is an essential part of measurement.

There is no point in measuring solely at the end of your campaign. If you do, you will be measuring in a vacuum of your own creation. It's necessary to begin measuring before or at the latest from the start of your campaign. Having a baseline gives you a basis against which to judge outcomes and should be your first actual measurement.

> **PRO TIP:** *Be careful not to over-burden your organization when undertaking measurement. Time, money, and people are limited resources.*

What to Measure

To adapt a quote attributed to Albert Einstein, "Not everything that matters can be measured and not everything that we can measure matters." You will not be able, or want to, measure every facet of your campaign.

Generally, I find that the 80/20 rule applies to measurement. Here's what I mean: 80 percent of what you measure applies to the vast majority of campaigns (for example, to improve awareness, raise revenue, and increase audience engagement). The other 20 percent is unique and specific to each campaign. Past client, Year Up, is a workplace-skills program whose goal is to increase the number of young people graduating from their program and getting jobs with corporate partners like Jet Blue and Google. The campaign's 80-percent goal was to create awareness of this opportunity among underserved communities while the 20-percent goal—specific to Year Up—was to increase leads, which in this case were represented by website visits from potential applicants to their program. Awareness levels and leads increased during the campaign due to the Influencer Effect generated by *Shark Tank*'s Daymond John's visit to Year Up's Los Angeles campus, and social media posts by basketball players Shaquille O'Neil and DeMar DeRozan. You can automatically track 80 percent of your measurement data by introducing a measurement system. As for the other 20 percent, you can use your creativity and available software or data to craft simple measurement solutions.

Despite sophisticated and varied ways to measure the Influencer Effect and your overall campaign, I prefer to simplify reporting by dividing results into two categories:

Tactical Impact Targets

Tactical impact targets are sometimes called outputs or activity metrics. These are short-term and process oriented. Reaching, increasing, and engaging your intended audience through social media, websites, email lists, events, ad-buys, and media mentions are all primary examples of tactical impact. Suppose the Influencer Effect increases your social media following by 5 percent, adds 10,000 sign-ups to your email list, and grows visits to your website 13 percent over your quarterly average. This data indicates increased engagement in your cause. Yet, unless these were your final goals, more social media followers or names on your mailing list are not an end in themselves.

Ultimate Impacts

Ultimate impact targets are sometimes referred to as outcomes or goals. More strategic than tactical impact targets, ultimate impact targets represent longer-term outcomes, and can tell you whether your campaign achieved its designated business, environmental, and social goals. Eradicating a disease, product introduction into new markets, and passing legislation are all examples of ultimate impacts. Suppose your company had signed the Fifteen Percent Pledge to devote 15% of your shelf space to Black-owned businesses and that through the Influencer Effect, product sales of sustainable products by your Black-owned brands grew by 24 percent. You would have hit certain of your business, environmental and social ultimate impact goals.

Nonprofits are self-evidently more focused on social impact goals than for-profits. Still, nonprofits cannot be effective without being well-run organizations, and that requires funding. To maintain funding, nonprofits must show strong ultimate impact metrics to their donor base. Say your campaign goal was to decrease the number of homeless people in your community. If your Influencer-led campaign raised $2.3 million to provide an additional thirty individuals or families with renovated accommodation, you achieved your ultimate impact target.

Tactical impact is more straightforward to measure than ultimate impact, which can be complex and less directly attributable. The mission of the African Wildlife Foundation (AWF) is to "ensure wildlife and wild lands thrive in modern Africa." Despite doing great work, AWF cannot accomplish this mission alone. AWF's efforts need community, business, media, civil society, and government cooperation both on the African continent and off. AWF measures its ultimate impact through rigorous and focused metric methods, and has recorded gains in wildlife protection, land conservation, and sustainable tourism.

Setting yourself up for success in your campaign and preparing as completely as you can to measure your tactical and ultimate impact targets will get you far. However, life happens. Sometimes, your campaign will be negatively affected by some uncontrollable external force such as an economic downturn or pandemic. In your final analysis, report whatever metrics you can, and explain the circumstances in which they arose.

A combination of tactical and ultimate impact target measurements makes for a potent and persuasive combination. To measure these, you need key performance indicators (KPIs). KPIs can include the resources you use, processes you employ, timelines, what's produced, and impacts. If you relate the data you are measuring to your KPIs, you will be able to see your campaign health. A KPI showing a 3 percent increase in online purchases over three months is simple to measure and is a barometer of growth. By establishing and regularly reviewing KPIs, you focus on what is important and can make informed decisions.

Let's take a closer look at many of the KPIs that help you measure your progress towards your tactical and ultimate impact targets. While not a comprehensive list, these are many of the main KPIs, and you will find others at goodinfluence-book.com.

Tactical Impact KPIs

Some folks see tactical impacts as ends in and of themselves, but actually, tactical impacts tend to show the milestones on the road to your goals. That stated, the insights gleaned from tracking your tactical impact targets can be tremendously valuable. Determine which tactical impact KPIs you can use from the below, reasonably-comprehensive list or create your own that are specific to your campaign:

Number of Influencers

The number of Influencers who support your campaign is an excellent indicator of buy-in if they provide their services for free. Of course, it isn't always a matter of more equals better. Certain factors such as the geographical breadth and length of your campaign are determinants of the number of Influencers who will engage. For the "End Polio Now" campaign, which lasted several years, there were over eighty ambassadors from all around the world. Alternatively, in our campaign for Washington, D.C. statehood, where the geographical area and duration was much more limited, with the campaign lasting less than four months, we had eight Influencers who engaged.

In both cases, tracking this tactical impact KPI showed the Influencer Effect had, to varying degrees, been successful.

On the brand side, companies pay Influencers for their support of a commercial or even a cause-related campaign, so the number of Influencers engaged in a campaign is a less meaningful tactical impact KPI. Business will by its raison-d'être have different KPIs from nonprofits. There is a growing trend with many corporate campaigns today to hire several micro or nano Influencers rather than one macro Influencer to reach local or ultra-precise audience segments. While their follower count will be far less, if your objective is to generate organic word-of-mouth, a measurable KPI you may want to follow is the micro Influencer route.

Draw KPIs from the criteria used to identify Influencers in the chapter about research, including the Influencer's match with your audience, geographical location, and trust levels.

Engagement

When looking at Influencers, one of the main criteria is whether the Influencer Effect generates engagement, and if so, how much and at what cost.

During the 2020 coronavirus pandemic, there was a rapid rise in online events. KPIs for tracking the tactical impacts of online events could include KPIs such as the number of people attending an event, the duration of audience interest, level of engagement, when they watch, how often, who is chatting, and about what.

Cost of Influencer Engagement

Commercial campaigns have differing levels of Influencer cost depending on the campaign. When launching "Exfoliating Body Polish" in Canada, Dove engaged fifty nano Influencers. They offered products and cash to post ads, add links, and otherwise talk about the product to their followers. This approach allowed Dove to hyper-focus on an audience and create word of mouth or buzz about their product. The fifty Instagram posts by the fifty nano Influencers had a total reach of 435,190 people, and their high 6.44 percent engagement rate resulted in over 28,000 engagements, bringing their final cost per engagement down to $0.14, a significantly lower cost when compared to their regular advertising campaigns. Not only that, but the audience was exactly the one Dove wanted to reach.[33]

Events

Tactical impact KPIs include the host's status vis-à-vis desired audience, attendance levels, Q&A interaction, and the benefits of attending (e.g., networking or fulfilling a professional qualification). For example, at a conference by The Royal Society, scientist, professor, and former musician Brian Cox,

---

33. This tactical impact KPI example was not a cause-based marketing campaign, but could easily be applied to any CSR campaign or for a nonprofit campaign where funds would otherwise be spent on promotion.

a UK media personality, will attract a large general audience. However, if your targeted audience is academics, Roger Penrose, the winner of the 2020 Nobel Prize in Physics, is a more robust choice and will give you a better KPI.

Website Traffic

Website traffic is an important metric because it indicates awareness, audience responsiveness, and engagement levels. You can assign the following KPIs to your campaign to track the Influencer Effect:

- Website users during the campaign, compared to before:
  - total users per month/week/day
  - total new site users
  - total unique new sessions on a specific section or page

- Website traffic acquisition sources
  - origin of the website visitors and the number of visitor sessions derived from specific campaign methods

- Website user behavior
  - session duration on the website
  - most viewed page(s)
  - bounce rate (leaving the site after visiting one page)
  - gender, age, location, and helpful affinity categories
  - goal conversion around specific actions you want users to take (e.g., clicking on a "give now" link)

> **Pro Tip:** *Google Analytics can show you the platforms like Facebook and Twitter that drove traffic to your site. It can also show gender, age, and other helpful affinity categories. This information means you can focus your efforts on where you are getting the most traction or those platforms where your target audience can be found.*

Email Engagement and List Building

If you want your Influencer Effect to drive people to sign up for your email list, measure the size of your list before and after the campaign. However, keep in mind that size isn't everything; engagement is critical. While my email list is several thousand people deep, it used to be three times larger. I culled it, removing bad email addresses or subscribers who hadn't engaged or opened one of my emails in years. It's better to have a smaller, active, and engaged audience than a large number of uninterested people who delete or ignore your messages.

Helpful tactical impact KPIs for tracking the health of your email campaigns include:

- Growth rates
  - number of new subscribers per campaign and overall
  - rate of growth compared to prior growth rate over a similar time period
- Open rates (percentage of people who opened the email)
- Clickthrough rates (percentage of people who clicked on one or more of the links in the email)

- Conversion rates (total number and percentage of people who clicked a link and then completed an action that you've specified as important to your campaign. This could be as simple as forwarding the email or visiting your website, or more involved, like buying a product or donating.)

I have found that the most effective emails have an Influencer connection, combined with creative content linked to a current issue. For example, Entertain Impact's email for Women's History month linked to our blog highlighting four extraordinary women at different career stages working in philanthropy. The intended audience was the philanthropic community, so these Influencers were a perfect match. The blog was one of our most popular ever, and we surpassed our open rate and clickthrough rate KPIs.

Conversion Rates

For business and philanthropy alike, getting a person interested in and then converting them to take the desired action is a substantial victory. This action can be whatever you want that will move you towards your campaign's ultimate impact targets. Amongst the most common are donate, share, purchase, watch, read, or recommend.

Generally speaking, you measure your conversion rate by dividing the number of actions taken (such as signing a petition) by the number of, say, unique visitors to your website.

Another example would be, say, you own a high-end jewelry store that is consistently running marketing campaigns. For every one hundred unique visitors, three buy jewelry, so your conversion rate is 3 percent. If the store undertakes an Influencer-led marketing campaign and the number of buyers goes to four per one hundred customers, your conversion rate is 4 percent, or an increase of 33 percent.

Average e-commerce website conversion rates for visitors to buyers range from 2 percent to 3 percent.[34] The conversion rate from the Influencer Effect is generally higher provided you have the right Influencer. Conversion rates as high as 12.7 percent have been achieved in the financial services industry.[35] This rate can be even higher in the philanthropic field. Goodwill Industries' Influencer campaign, headed by Senior Director of PR Lauren Lawson-Zilai, generated "as high as 10 percent engagement rate amongst social media followers and a 30 percent conversion rate in turning prospects into Goodwill shoppers, donors, and ambassadors."[36] Of course, context plays a part, so if this rate was only achieved on Giving Tuesday, that would be an outlier that does not represent conversion rates for the rest of the year.

Bear in mind when setting and evaluating this KPI, you will gain valuable information if you are able to find out what made the consumer convert. Research what particular webpages or content are leading to people taking your desired action. Messaging can play a big part. For example, adding

---

34. Saleh, "Average Website Conversion Rate."
35. Raedts, "Conversion-Driven Influencer Campaigns."
36. Lawson-Zilai, "Cause Docs."

the words "every penny will help" to a donation request from the American Cancer Society increased giving by nearly double. Likewise, changing the cost of an item from $1,000 a year to $84 a month, or changing the category of a $5 fee from "shipping fee" to "a small $5 fee" will increase the number of consumers who take action.[37]

Media Coverage

Whether traditional or digital, media falls into three categories: owned, paid, and earned. Your choice of which media category to focus on will be determined by which of your targeted audience segments consume and react to each type.

- **Owned Media:** This is media you control, such as your website, blog, social media, magazine, and newsletter. The Influencer Effect is typically measured by engagement—specifically desirable comments, quotes, and shares. These metrics are available from those platforms you use to distribute your content.
- **Paid Media:** This is media you pay for, such as advertising. It can be ad words on Google, a radio commercial, banner ads, display ads, interstitial ads, and outdoor billboards. In all cases, you are buying eyeballs. While Influencers are used in commercials to promote products with consistently successful outcomes, I do not pay for

---

37. Ciotti, "Understanding Consumer Behavior."

their involvement in philanthropic campaigns and rarely for advertising to promote their involvement.

• **Earned Media:** Here, the media deems your campaign newsworthy and covers it at no cost. Earned media is my favorite type of media. An example of earned media was when I created a Multi-Pact by pairing RCA (pro bono), their artist Matthew Koma, and the National Eating Disorder Association to promote Matthew's single about his anorexia, entitled "Dear Ana." *People* magazine, along with newspapers and other media outlets, picked up the story. Matthew also made himself available for interviews and wrote a blog. All the publicity was free for all parties involved.

The cost of reaching your desired audience via earned media is one aspect of the Influencer Effect that can be a substantial saving. The online marketing resource Influencer Marketing Hub found the average earned media value was $5.87 for each $1 spent on Influencer marketing, a 587 percent return. As the Influencers I work with on philanthropic campaigns do not charge, the ROI is even higher.

Another study, this one based in the UK, looked at a European life science company's $7.5 million diabetes campaign that engaged for a fee a celebrity chef to reach 52,803 physicians. The cost in reaching their desired audiences using the Influencer Effect was $0.38 from earned media—compared to $0.51 from paid media—a 24 percent cost saving.[38]

---

38. Hofmann and Malhotra, "Pervasive Analytics."

While this study used real paid media costs, other campaigns use ad-equivalency as a proxy to determine the value of earned media versus paid advertising. For example, five posts by one macro and four micro Influencers for a 2021 Washington, D.C. statehood campaign run by the Entertain Impact Advocacy Alliance had an ad-equivalency of over $80,000, according to social media tracking tool Brand 24. For those organizations with an active Influencer ambassador program, over $1 million per annum in ad-equivalency is not unusual. To all this, I will add this warning: ad-equivalency can be dangerous to your credibility because it does not measure impact. Instead, it measures the cost-equivalent and impression count of what a paid ad might possibly deliver. The assumption here is that you would have bought such an advert, which is not by any means a given. If you had, would you have paid the full or discounted price? The price you would have paid directly correlates to your ad-equivalency value. In other words, the higher the price, the more earned media value. While I have clients that use or ask for ad-equivalency as a KPI, I suggest that you be cautious in adopting it as your primary tactical impact target, if at all.

Another set of earned media metrics has been created by the public relations industry. These include quantitative measures like the number or placement of mentions of your brand, number of unique stories, and media pitched. Qualitative measures used by PR agencies include message content, sentiment analysis, coverage of key issues or themes, and share of voice.

Numerous other examples and research findings can be found throughout this book and elsewhere that show how the Influencer Effect amplifies these PR metrics. You can check out the Coalition for Public Relations Research Standards,[39] the Institute for Public Relations,[40] or follow the "Queen of Measurement" Katie Delahaye Paine[41] for additional information by those far more expert than me.

Whether owned, paid, or earned media, coverage can be good, bad, or neutral, and there are several KPIs to measure this, including:

• Was the headline positive?
• Did it contain a desirable visual?
• Was there a third-party endorsement?
• Is your audience more likely to respond as a result?

Choose those that are important to your specific campaign.

Social Media Engagement

Influencers' reach, growth, impressions, and engagement are all determinants of their effectiveness, and setting these as your tactical impact targets is a good idea. Here's how it might look: an Influencer with 50 million followers with 3.4 percent actively engaged followers can deliver 1.7 million pairs of

39. Institute for Public Relations, "About Public Relations."
40. Visit https://instituteforpr.org/ for more information about the Institute for Public Relations.
41. The "Queen of Measurement" can be found at http://www.painepublishing.com/

eyeballs on your campaign. Suppose 30,000 of those people take the desired action as a result. This would be persuasive data for your social media engagement KPI.

Social media KPIs can also focus on the elements contained in a post, or the quality of the content. Here are some KPIs to consider:

- Was the content posted or mentioned by an Influencer?
- Did it include a visual?
- Did it include a hashtag?
- Was it in an authentic voice?
- Did it include a call to action?
- Did it convey authenticity?

TOP TOOLS

For your social media measurement, you can use services such as Sprout Social, HootSuite, Keyhole, or Brand 24. All measure, to varying degrees, brand and cause mentions across social platforms, news, blogs, videos, forums, podcasts, reviews, and more. However, not all tools measure all things, so make sure you can get measured what you need when choosing one. You'll find more information and suggestions at goodinfluencebook.com.

Raising Awareness

Raising awareness is, in my experience, the number one objective of Influencer-led campaigns. Whether you are a one-person band, Disney, or UNICEF, you want to be noticed and loved, and to differentiate yourself from your competitors. As set out throughout this book, academic and business research has proven that the Influencer Effect raises an organization or campaign's profile. The numerous Influencers who participated in the "Diabetes Dance Dare" campaign for the American Diabetes Association raised awareness of ways to control or prevent the disease while simultaneously elevating the visibility of the organization itself. The campaign far exceeded the targets for its awareness KPIs: posts garnered over a billion impressions, the announcement got over one hundred media pickups, and tens of thousands of people liked, shared, and commented on social media about the campaign.

Raising Support

The Influencer Effect may have created awareness for your brand or cause, but did your desired audience respond to support your brand or cause? Again, there are many ways to ascertain this: How many sign-ups did you get to your email list? How many people shared the information about your campaign with peers? How many people became members, volunteers, or customers?

I worked for the Environmental Defense Fund in integrating Influencers into the creation of the "Moms Clean Air Force" campaign. The goal was to protect children from high toxic mercury levels. Layla Ali, Blyth Danner, and Julianne Moore all backed the campaign to get 100,000 moms to contact their local congressperson to support the clean air regulations brought in by the Obama administration. Ultimately, over 129,000 moms did so, and the clean air regulations became law despite challenges from dirty coal. The campaign was such a success that today the Moms Clean Air Force is an independent nonprofit organization with over one million parents protecting their children's health by uniting against air and climate pollution.

KPIs tracking support will depend to an extent on your Activation and call to action. Made in Memphis Entertainment (MIME) is a Black-owned start-up music group launched in 2015 by Hall of Fame songwriter David Porter and serial entrepreneur Tony Alexander. I am deeply involved with MIME as a board member and senior advisor. MIME, which consists of a distribution company, record label, recording studios, music publishing, and music for visual media, was created with a social mission. This mission is to bring music back to Memphis and to give opportunities to young people from under-resourced communities—primarily BIPOC. MIME can measure support for its mission in several ways, including the quality of news media the organization generates, the number of local businesses, universities, and other community partners who support MIME, the number of industry associations that recognize their work, and the number of BIPOC young people who become interns and employees. I am happy to report that MIME is making impressive progress as measured by all these KPIs, with women comprising half of the organization's leadership and three-fourths of the company's employees being people of color.

Raising Revenue

The Influencer Effect boosts businesses by connecting products to audiences and converting them to buyers. We have seen the stock price and revenue increase when Influencers engage to boost a brand. Revenue KPIs are relatively simple to measure and attribute. For nonprofits, a direct appeal by an Influencer can produce measurable results in the form of donations. Lin-Manuel Miranda, the creator of *Hamilton*, partnered with the educational organization Flamboyan Foundation to help revitalize the arts in Puerto Rico post-Hurricane Maria. *Hamilton*'s seventeen-day run in Puerto Rico raised nearly $15 million from ticket sales and contributions to a new arts fund. Lin-Manuel also took part in a contest on Omaze, where for a $10 ticket, you had the chance to go to Puerto Rico and see *Hamilton* with him. This lottery raised an additional $1M for the cause.

One of the desired goals for any philanthropic campaign is to create more and varied donors. Rapper-turned-country-singer Kid Rock supported my "Canine Companions for Independence" Veterans Day campaign. He and other Influencers brought in new donors at a significantly higher rate than prior years' campaigns. Academic research supports this by showing that an Influencer endorsement gives a "celebrity bump," thereby increasing contributions and lowering fundraising costs.[42]

---

42. Harris and Ruth, "Value of Celebrity Affiliation," 945-967.

Awareness, support, and revenue raised are relatively straightforward to measure. With increases in these three KPIs, a business can undertake more R&D, hire more employees, buy new equipment, return profits to their shareholders, and expand philanthropic programs. For a nonprofit, you can do most of the above plus fulfill your mission, whether that's providing vaccines, feeding the hungry, or reducing climate change.

Specific organizations may see these three goals as ultimate impact, but I generally see them as tactical, although raising revenues could be considered ultimate impact for a business. In the final analysis, it doesn't matter what category they fit into. What is important is to determine if they are relevant to you and, of course, that you measured them.

Ultimate Impact KPIs

The interconnectedness of our world means many factors come into play when determining if ultimate impact was achieved and by whom. It would not be very smart for me to suggest that every campaign we work on has a substantial impact on the long-term mission of our clients. Many other factors and players come into play. However, our agency and the campaigns we run do contribute at different levels to our clients' work. For example, the Influencer Effect has raised hundreds of thousands for Saint Damien Pediatric Hospital in Haiti, paying for treatments for hundreds of people and covering staff overheads. These represent ultimate impact. However, when India went polio-free, I didn't have access to the data to precisely attribute the Rotary Polio Ambassador campaign as being directly responsible to this incredible outcome. How do you look at this contribution from one campaign versus the decades of efforts by multiple players, especially the Indian government, the international community, Rotary, UNICEF, the Bill and Melinda Gates Foundation, local health workers, and so many more? Perhaps our Bollywood actors drove vaccination rates up by a percent or two, but this is purely a guess. Our campaign was but a grain of sand on the beach, and that's satisfaction enough in this case. You can't be perfect about measurement; you do what you can.

Return on Investment

Return on investment (ROI) calculates how much revenue you earned for every dollar spent, with the aim being to make more money than you invested. For business, ROI is considered to be one KPI category of ultimate impact. In the nonprofit world, this KPI is perhaps less important—I get asked for the ROI not so much by nonprofit Chief Marketing Officers (CMOs), but by Chief Financial Officers (CFOs). While there is more to ultimate impact measurement than ROI, it's a fact of life that organizations need to generate revenues and justify where money is spent. I get it. Sometimes ROI includes an allocation for staff costs, although I have found that many CFOs treat that figure as a sunk cost and do not include it. Instead, they opt to include only third-party charges, including, of course, my agency's fees.

Sample ROI Memo

While creating a budget for the next fiscal year for a nonprofit client, I drafted a memo on ROI that the CMO gave to the CFO with examples from several prior campaigns illustrating the dollar value of the Influencer Effect. Below is a condensed version of what I sent to the CMO. You will recognize several of these examples from the book, so I have referenced the organization's name and campaign rather than repeat the details. Please feel free to use these real examples to convince your own stakeholders of the value of the Influencer Effect.

To: CMO

From: PK

Re: ROI

Here are bullet points on the impact of Influencer-led campaigns I've participated in with other organizations. Some include ambassadors deeply involved over time while others engaged Influencers on a one-off basis. I hope these can aid your discussions internally as you decide whether to move forward with running your own Influencer-led campaign.

Funds Raised
- **Many campaigns see increases in individual donors.** One example includes Best Friends Animal Society, which added monthly donors to their base.
- **Increase in money raised due to renewed enthusiasm generated by the Influencer campaign.** Rotary membership raised $75 million for the "End Polio Now" campaign.
- **Funding saved or increased by governments, NGOs, and foundations.** One example is the $5.1 billion raised for vaccines for GAVI involving the Gates Foundation's "Art of Saving a Life" campaign.

- **One-off major gifts.** For example, an individual anonymous gift of $400K was made to Saint Damien's Pediatric Hospital Haiti.
- **Influencers consistently donate to the cause, whether publicly announced or gifts made anonymously.** For example, Ryan Reynolds and Blake Lively give to hunger organizations, Will and Jada Pinkett Smith give to youth development, and Dan Whitney (Larry the Cable Guy) gives to children's hospitals.

Media and Advertising
- **Earned media.** The value of earned media can be worth hundreds of thousands of dollars. An example discussed earlier in the book includes Rotary Polio Ambassadors.

Cost Savings
- **Reduced litigation costs** by over six figures. Substantial litigation costs were not incurred as a result of public pressure sparked by an Influencer campaign—the "American Monuments Alliance" campaign called on the Trump administration to reverse their order to permit drilling on National Monuments.
- **Lower fundraising costs.** A research study entitled the "Analysis of the Value of Celebrity Affiliation to Nonprofit Contributions" by Erica Harris and Julie Ruth found that celebrity affiliation has a substitution effect such that fundraising expenses are lower.[43]

Partnership opportunities
- **Broadcast partnerships.** For example, Kevin and Eve hosted the CBS show *Play On—Celebrating The Power of Music To Make Change* which resulted in $7.3M being raised for Why Hunger and the NAACP Legal and Educational Defense Fund.

43. Harris and Ruth, "Value of Celebrity Affiliation," 1–23.

Non-financial Impacts
- **Reduce the average age of donors.** Several campaigns are examples of this, such as preserving Nina Simone's childhood home.
- **Increase employee pride.** The "Diabetes Dance Dare" campaign by the American Diabetes Association is an example.
- **Grow membership enthusiasm.** Rotary's "End Polio Now" is a great example of reigniting excitement in a long-term initiative.
- **Attract millennials and Gen Z to work at your organization.** Most campaigns will do this.
- **Open doors for senior leadership,** such as increasing their invitations to speak. The March of Dimes ran a campaign that led to a high-profile speaking engagement.
- **Reach new audiences,** including potential supporters, stakeholders, and targets. Several campaigns throughout this book from animal welfare to international health show this outcome.

You can see a strong ROI in these examples, and the expenses are low since Influencers, at least the ones we work with, do not charge. You can also see plenty of benefits that are not hard dollars but in-kind donations or even more esoteric in nature. I hope that this helps your CFO determine the Influencer Effect's value proposition.

> **Pro Tip:** *Give your CFO the whole spectrum of value that your campaign achieved such as program outcomes, not just the financial ones.*

Of course, you cannot directly attribute all financial contributions to Influencers, but they play their part in driving donations. When the Bill and Melinda Gates Foundation had a vaccine conference and raised several billion dollars, there was no direct correlation with the eighty "End Polio Now" Rotary Ambassadors. These Influencers played a part in raising awareness with governments, NGOs, businesses, and the public. Let's assume, hypothetically, that the Influencer Effect accounted for 0.1 percent of the overall efforts to raise awareness, support, and revenues. This would mean that of the $4.5 billion raised collectively over three years, $4.5 million could be attributed to the participation of the Rotary ambassador campaign. That is undoubtedly a subjective assumption, but I use it to illustrate the indirect benefits of the Influencer Effect and how it plays into and amplifies broader efforts.

You can also compare the ROI across your organization's campaigns to determine what works best. For example, one of my first clients, an environmental organization, found at the time that a photo and quote from Senator John McCain achieved the best donor response rate and ROI, followed by a polar bear.

On average, my campaign's direct ROI is conservatively in the range of around 1:8 to 1:12 during the campaign, and even more if you take into account the several months following the end of a campaign or the non-financial benefits.

Social Return on Investment

The social return on investment, or the SROI, is a measurement of your societal impact. This is relevant to your stakeholders, especially donors or investors, who are on the lookout for how your organization is impacting the greater good. Like a traditional ROI, you can assign a monetary value to your social, economic, and environmental impact.

> Use this formula to calculate your SROI:
> SROI = the social benefits divided by total investment

For example, if over a five-year period, your organization invested $50,000 in a marketing campaign and over, say, the next five years, future income flows derived from that campaign, discounted to today's value, equal $125,000, then the SROI is 2.5. Meaning that for every $1 invested upfront, the financial present-day value is $2.50.

Year Up, which participated in a 2021 Pathways for Advancing Careers and Education study,[44] is a good example of how to calculate SROI. Over a five-year review period, the results were that for every $1 invested in Year Up programs, the societal benefits such as reductions in public assistance, financial hardship, and debt reduction were worth $2.46. Additionally, the study showed that Year Up graduates working full-time had average annual earnings 28 percent ($1,895) higher than the control group, and the net gain to society was $32,328 per participant. What is not measured, but is equally important, is the generational impact and the reduction in trauma or stress that these programs deliver to their participants.

---

44. Fein, David and Samuel Dastrup. 2022. *Benefits that Last: Long-Term Impact and Cost-Benefit Findings for Year Up.* OPRE Report 2022-77. Washington, DC: Office of Planning, Research, and Evaluation, Administration for Children and Families, U.S. Department of Health and Human Services.

How to arrive at Social Impact Value is a subject in its own right, and you will find resources on the book's website. Legitimately demonstrating your SROI is valuable to all facets of your organization.

Culture

My theory of change consists of first moving the culture in a different direction, leading to behavior change, and finally to policy change, often in a loop. Popular culture changes society, and I repeat this daily nearly as often as the devotees of the Gayatri mantra. That's 108 times every morning and evening.

As discussed in these pages, the Influencer Effect has played a substantial role in changing attitudes towards climate change, gay rights, racial justice, and more. The Norman Lear Center at USC's Media Impact Project[45] is "a hub for collecting, developing and sharing approaches for measuring the impact of media, aiming to understand better the role that media plays in changing knowledge, attitudes, and behavior among individuals and communities." Its report "Africa in the Media," produced with Criss Cross Global, highlighted that Africa or Africans are rarely seen on popular US television shows or in the news, and when they are, then it is often in a negative light.[46] Other Lear Center reports suggest that by creating entertainment content closer to reality, people's

45. Visit the website Norman Lear Center Projects for more about this initiative. https://learcenter.org/project/media-impact-project/
46. Blakley et al., "Africa in the Media."

bias against Africa will change. A follow-up report would be helpful to see if change has happened. Changing people's perceptions is a valuable ultimate impact KPI.

Behavior Change

If you can change people's perceptions, you can change their behavior, and then you have a shot at changing the world. Fortunately, the Influencer Effect encourages, amplifies, and accelerates behavior change. Getting a person to behave in a way they've never considered before is, in fact, the power of the Influencer Effect.

Rapper Logic's song "1-800-273-8255" (the National Suicide Prevention Lifeline number) brought awareness to the issue of suicide and highlighted the NSPL's hotline. This immensely popular 2017 song has had over 1.2 billion streams, and its video showing a struggling teenager who calls the hotline a further 425 million views. A study in the British Medical Journal used Twitter to gauge the amount of attention the song received. They measured the period beginning thirty-four days before the song's initial release through the live performances of the song at the 2017 MTV Video Music Awards and the 2018 Grammy Awards. The study concluded that the suicide hotline received 9,915—or 6.9 percent—more calls, and suicides declined by 245—or 5.5 percent—over that period versus equivalent prior periods. The study's lead author, Thomas Niederkrotenthaler, stated the song had been the "broadest and most sustained suicide prevention messaging directly connected to a story of hope and recovery." I would postulate that additional factors played a significant role in the campaign's beneficial outcomes, including the power of wrapping up a serious subject in an entertaining package for public consumption, and the strong connection that Logic—along with featured performers Alessia Kara and Khalid—had with the desired audience.[47]

Brands measure customer behavior in several ways, including many of those already discussed. Other factors are specific to the sector, like traffic increases per store, average per-customer spending, and product purchase changes.

Other examples of behavior change KPIs—taken from a sampling of campaigns created or managed by Entertain Impact—include the increased time parents spend talking with their children, mathematic organizations engaged in a specific subject, and reductions in selfies that make wild animals suffer.

Policy Change

By changing policy, you can change the game for the long term, whether it's your condominium's management rules or an act of Congress.

Global Citizen has used the Influencer Effect extensively to support, encourage, and cajole culture, behavior, and policy change. Global Citizen's annual Central Park concerts and others worldwide are themed around social issues such as poverty, education, and vaccine equity, and are embraced by

---

47. Kaufman, "Saved Hundreds of Lives."

a Who's Who of Influencers. Global Citizen concerts, with substantial Influencer involvement as presenters and performers, have resulted in significant awareness among younger generations who undertake specific actions to gain a ticket. Per the organization's website, in 2021, its Global Citizens have taken nearly 30 million actions, impacted 1.09 billion lives, and contributed to $35.4 billion in funds subsequently distributed by governments and other civil society organizations. These actions via Global Citizen campaigns have, for example, helped companies improve their supply chain practices to include more women-owned businesses, and encouraged governments to eliminate neglected tropical diseases in Africa.

You can measure how the Influencer Effect results in ultimate impact. For the Environmental Defense Fund, I had several Influencers support cap-and-trade legislation designed to reduce US greenhouse omissions. The 2007 bill passed the House for the first time, but alas was never brought to the floor of the Senate. Passing the House can be considered KPI data for this campaign and a milestone measurement towards the ultimate impact target of passing climate change legislation. In this example, you could also measure the tactical impacts, such as the number of people who signed a pledge, whether or not staffers know of your cause, and the number of co-sponsors to the bill.

Policy-oriented campaigns—such as climate change, artistic rights, and get out the vote—are among the most challenging but meaningful campaigns I have worked on. Even a partial victory can pave the way for change in the future.

Unexpected Consequences

Setting goals is essential, but you cannot predict everything. There have been positive consequences to campaigns I have co-built with my clients that were complete surprises. While unforeseen consequences were not part of the original plan, that doesn't mean they were not valuable or worth measuring!

For the American Diabetes Association's "Diabetes Dance Dare" campaign, with tens of Influencers participating, the unintended consequence was that the employees' and volunteers' work was recognized. This acknowledgment generated pride in the organization and motivation to continue the work. These factors were not anticipated but were easy to see from social media posts to the upbeat vibe in the workplace. Fortunately, all my campaigns' unintended consequences have been constructive so far. I attribute this to well-researched, planned, and executed campaigns, along with a dash of kismet.

In the final analysis, ultimate impact is why we do the work, so to be able to identify, measure, and interpret the consequences of that work is rewarding and motivating.

> ### *Top Tools*
> *Other KPIs to measure tactical and ultimate impact will be available at* goodinfluencebook.com.

How to Measure

Before you start measuring, I'd suggest you review your goals, determine what insights you want to get from the data, and consider how you will implement lessons learned. Social Value International, a member organization focused on social impact and social value, has seven principles that are a helpful way to think about how to measure your campaign.[48] They can be summarized as:

- Involve your stakeholders.
- Understand how change is created.
- Value what matters, including only material information.
- Do not exaggerate the results.
- Be transparent.
- Have a third party verify your results.

If your measurement protocols adhere, at least in part, to these principles, then you will be doing an admirable job.

Designate Team Members

Measurement is a collaborative process. You need to agree on your goals, audience, KPIs, benchmarks, tools, and budget. You then need to determine, collect, analyze, and find insights from the data you've agreed to collect.

---

48. Social Value International, "Principles of Social Value."

Who collects your data is an important decision. Do you do it internally or externally? There are pros and cons for both. If you don't have a team, then consider hiring external expertise. These specialists likely know more than you do and don't add to your fixed overhead. When hiring a consultant, you need to specify, in detail, the deliverables, budget, and timeline. The more specific you can be, the better the outcome. For those smaller companies and nonprofits, I recommend an individual consultant or small firm as the way to go, coupled with a training plan so your in-house team can take over these responsibilities in due course. Remember, there is always the possibility of finding pro bono or voluntary help in measurement via your local network, or if you are a nonprofit, going to a variety of organizations that support this work, such as DataKind. Whichever way you go, I'd suggest you make one person on your team responsible for data collection, although preferably any team member who touches a data point should participate and be knowledgeable about measurement.

Determine What Represents Your Goals

Your KPI choices need to be manageable, relate back to your goals, and be relevant to your stakeholders.

Ask yourself, "What choice of KPIs will show me that we made progress towards or achieved our goal?" Suppose your primary goal is to increase unaided awareness (i.e., audiences knowing your brand without any prompts or reminders) by 5 percent over three months. One metric that can indicate tactical impact and progress can be the quantity and quality of press coverage that mentions your brand. For ultimate impact, performing a pre/post survey of your audience will give you evidence of whether the awareness rate changed over that period.

Weight Your Metrics

Once you have determined the appropriate proxies, you add a value to each to prioritize them. For example, if your goal is to increase online sales, a new visitor to your website may be worth three times more than a person reading about your brand in the press.

Katie Paine of Paine Publishing, who advises Entertain Impact on measurement, recommends creating a Quality Index around a group of specific KPIs. Each individual metric has a plus or minus tally based on various scenarios. For example, if your KPI is getting high-quality media coverage, a plus scenario worth three points is, "Did the coverage contain one or more positive messages?" Deduct three points for something you do not want to see in the media, such as, "the coverage contains one or more negative messages." You then total up the plus/minus columns to see if you have a positive index score. Examples of indexes can be found on this book's website.

Benchmarking

A benchmark is a measurement you compare the Influencer Effect against to determine your progress. Classic benchmarking categories are prior performance or your competitors, but mainly you implement what your stakeholders will find important.

It will be necessary for you to establish a baseline to benchmark your performance against. You need to know where you started before knowing if you ended up in a better place. At a minimum, take your first measurement before your campaign starts. Say your baseline shows that before your campaign, you had a monthly growth rate of one hundred new Instagram followers with an average age of fifty years old, and an acquisition cost of $5 per follower. This data allows you to benchmark your campaign against future activity. Subsequently, you measure that during your Influencer-led campaign, your Instagram followers increased by two hundred per month, had an average age of forty-five years, and it cost you $2.50 per new follower. Therefore, you can conclude that your campaign attracted younger followers at twice the regular monthly average and at half the cost. This information is valuable to present to your board, senior management, and to know yourself.

For certain campaigns, you will measure at the beginning, along the way, at the end, and possibly again after a more extended period to see if the changes you instigated sustained. By measuring during the duration of your campaign, rather than waiting until it's over, you can adjust your campaign tactics to give you a better chance of strong outcomes.

Collect Your Data

Don't forget that you are probably not the first to measure whatever you are measuring. There may be a mass of publicly available information you can use. And it doesn't hurt to check out the competition's research to see what they are doing. When I find another organization has already measured ahead of me, I may be able to use their data or, at the very least, benchmark my campaign against their findings.

You have a varied array of measurement possibilities and tools. Choose the ones that make sense for your campaign, organization, purpose, timelines, and budget. Much data, such as social media, can be collected while sitting at your computer. However, I like to go where the action is and interact with people. They tell stories that cause us to have emotional reactions. This human response can be as powerful for your stakeholders as hard facts.

Determine if you want to use quantitative (statistics) and/ or qualitative (stories) methods. While both are robust methodologies, I see quantitative reporting as data for the head, and qualitative reporting as data for the heart. Basically, the difference between how many tubes of Marvis toothpaste you buy a year versus why you love the brand. Funders and investors tend to want the hard facts and figures, while the public responds more to emotional content. You need to use both to succeed.

You'll also need to consider when the information is required. For campaigns you'll want to collect data weekly or monthly, present no less than quarterly for management meetings, and every six months at a minimum for boards.

Collecting or mining data is one thing, but the quality of the data is quite another. Determine carefully, just as you do with the food you eat, where your data comes from. Poor quality food will ruin your health, and poor quality data will ruin your understanding of your campaign's effectiveness. Good data is like bread—best when it is fresh. Given the rapid delivery of information in the last few years, data gets old and stale very quickly. It is easy to spend a small fortune on measurement and not end up with anything useful. You can collect your data by a variety of methods. Below are the main ones.

Surveys

A survey can collect masses of data efficiently. It consists primarily of a combination of closed, ranked, or open-ended questions. Surveys aren't typically done in person unless using the interview format. These are basically quantitative interviews that ask a set number of structured questions, usually to a larger number of participants, and can be relatively easy, cheap, and speedy to pull off. They are increasingly being done online since people are reluctant to pick up the phone and participate. However, the information can be superficial if the questions are not formed well. Here are examples of the three types of survey questions:

- closed questions (e.g., Which brand do you prefer, Gucci or Channel?)
- perception questions—on a scale of 1 to 5, with 5 being totally agree and 1 being totally disagree, to what extent do you agree or disagree with this statement (e.g., Gucci handbags are a status symbol.)
- open-ended questions need to be manually tallied, adding time and money to the analysis of responses. (e.g., What do you think of Gucci's new handbag?)

Generally, survey results are relatively easy to report, are ordinarily cost-effective, scalable, and easy to administer. A 2017 study entitled "The Effectiveness of Celebrities in Conservation Marketing" in the UK published in PloS One[49] used interviews and online surveys for a hypothetical marketing campaign. The campaign compared the public's willingness to engage and recall conservation messages in adverts using David Beckham, naturalist Chris Packham, or Prince William versus a control group. Outcomes revealed that participants were more likely to engage if an Influencer was involved, although message recall was worse than non-celebrity adverts. Additionally, the authors determined that conservation marketing organizations do not assess the effectiveness of the Influencers they use.

49. Duthie et al., "The Effectiveness of Celebrities."

Whether you pay for an Influencer or not, consider whether you measure your individual Influencer's effectiveness and what KPIs to use to do so. One KPI for the Influencer Effect is which Influencer is more persuasive with the general public. Incidentally, in this study, Prince William was nearly three times more effective than the control group in persuading people to get involved.

The disadvantage of surveys is that the quality of the data can be contentious if the questions are confusing or the organization undertaking the research does not adhere to certain professional standards such as those laid down by the Insights Association.[50] Always test your survey first on a small sample of recipients to make sure you are going to get the answers you need.

Qualitative Interviews

Qualitative, face-to-face interviews are more time-consuming and expensive to do than surveys.

Qualitative interviews have a set list of questions and tend to be open-ended, wide-ranging, and unstructured. This approach means answers tend to be more extended, in-depth, and individualized. For "The Global Boyhood Initiative," a Promundo and Kering Foundation campaign on raising emotionally healthy boys, I hired research firm Perry Undem. They interviewed fourteen boys across the United States from

50. Insight Association, "Code of Standards."

diverse geographical, political, and gender backgrounds. Out of their excellent research came insights about the state of boys and the campaign's theme and concept.

A subset or interview technique is active listening, where you intentionally prepare to listen, do so attentively, understand what's being said, and provide feedback so that the interview subject feels there is respect and engagement. Hearing and conveying stories can be very powerful. These stories help you understand what's going on in-depth, and you can extrapolate from them. Listening—whether it's to Jack Saul recording military vets for his Moral Injury Public Listening Project or Ford interviewing owners as to why they like their car—makes room for learning much more than interpreting a data set of mere numbers. Active listening is different than straight observation, which is where you observe your subject and report. I don't use that approach for hard data. Observation is a helpful tool used respectfully for anecdotal stories or visuals. For example, this is a powerful approach for Make-A-Wish when they arrange for an Influencer—John Cena, Justin Bieber, and Michael Jordan being amongst the champion wish givers—to visit a sick child in person.

Whichever way you choose to go—and resources often determine this—surveying and interviews give you results, insights and sparks ideas.

> **Pro Tip:** *Use online tools like Zoom to record your interviews. Video, if possible, is preferable, although using it can affect the outcome as people can become inhibited and clam up.*

Focus Groups

In a focus group, you sit down with a group of people to get their reactions to your content, Activations, or campaign. Movie studios regularly have pre-release movie screenings for focus groups costing thousands of dollars. After getting the focus group's input, endings are changed and scenes reshot. The information from focus groups tends to be fairly detailed, yet is quicker and cheaper than one-on-one interviews. Negatives for focus groups generally include one of the following: one or more participants potentially having an outsized impact on the group, the work of finding the participants, and the challenge of securing interviewers who know what they are doing. During the Covid-19 pandemic, when case numbers were ticking up, many focus group surveys were conducted online via a conference system like Zoom.

Big Data

Vast swaths of complex public data are often available. Finding a trend in that data can give you a competitive advantage. If Gen Alpha's gaming use is 30 percent higher than Gen Z's, then reach this demographic by working with Twitch gamers.

> **TOP TOOLS**
>
> *Numerous tools can aid you in measuring your campaign. You can survey your network using Google Forms or can ask one of the online survey companies like PickFu or Survey Monkey to provide a panel representing your desired audiences.*

Interpret and Evaluate Your Data

Interpretation is what you discern about a situation from the data. Evaluation determines whether the program has been a success or not. In just three months in 2021, the World Health Organization Foundation's "Go Give One" campaign raised $1.7 million, thereby matching and exceeding the ELMA Vaccines & Immunization Foundation's $1 million matching grant. At $5 per vaccine, this resulted in 540,000 additional COVID-19 vaccines being made available to those who needed them most in countries that could not afford them. These are relatively definitive numbers and leave little room for interpretation. The WHO Foundation and ELMA's evaluation would likely conclude that the campaign was a resounding success and a building block for the future.

When evaluating your data, keep in mind that there is often an element of interpretation as you draw conclusions. Consider these types of questions when looking at data:

• Was there a change in the outcomes and impacts due to the campaign?

- Were there any unintended consequences, and what caused them?
- What was the economic, environmental, and social impact of the campaign?
- What were my worst responses? (You learn more from failure than you do from success, so sort responses from worst to best to reveal more interesting insights.)
- Which element of the campaign generated the most results over time?
- Is there a lag time for certain tactics?

The Charles and Lynn Schusterman Family Philanthropies constructed a helpful framework for interpreting data.[51] To summarize, you look at the facts, stats, and trends. Be a detective when analyzing your data. Look for a clue, pattern, or theme that gives you an "aha" moment. Data can show you what soccer moms are buying in specific malls at certain times or which age group of diabetic patients does not take their medicines after six weeks without a reminder. You can see if these trends changed year on year, or whether specific patterns emerged.

Data interpretation without context can be misleading. XFM, the first London indie radio station—owned by Chris Parry, the founder of Fiction Records—had a fantastic marketing campaign around its launch. Unfortunately, it debuted on-air the day Princess Diana died in a car accident. The launch was a categorical failure purely from a data perspective,

51. Kaplowitz, "Data Playbook."

but when considering the extraordinary circumstances, one wouldn't necessarily draw that conclusion.

By comparing your current campaign to your prior ones or to third-party campaigns, you can glean many insights. I look at social media post engagement rates of various Influencers versus other Influencers within the same campaign, and how those rates stack up against other campaigns and forms of marketing or communications.

Be wary of letting interpretation slip into manipulation. Don't brag and overinflate the results of your campaign. When challenged, you will lose credibility, and your other outcomes may be viewed with suspicion. Be accurate and, if anything, err on the side of caution and understatement. Even in cases of great success, directly attributing change solely to your campaign is problematic. Take the US-based ELMA Music Foundation which funds music programs in youth community centers under the Music & Youth Development Alliance banner. These programs attract young people into local youth community centers which then also provide wrap-around services such as education, health, and immigration. Data shows that young people from these centers stay in school, do better academically, and exhibit positive social behavior. It would be great to attribute all this progress to the music programs, but that would not be true. The major contributing factors to these outcomes include the wrap-around services, family support, teacher involvement, and after-school programs.

On the other hand, one outcome that the ELMA Music Foundation has been able to claim as directly attributable to their programming is the measurable social-emotional development these participating young people demonstrate. ELMA's multi-year ongoing study has shown marked improvement in confidence, peer-to-peer cooperation, self-awareness, self-management, responsible decision making, and relationship skills. When looking at behavior change—or for that matter, assessing your progress towards any goal—make sure you can attribute specific contributions or outcomes to your campaign before making any claims.

One final example of interpreting and evaluating data. The ELMA Music Foundation can show that the South Central Los Angeles Music & Youth Development Alliance member, A Place Called Home, has 95 percent of its members graduate high school on time in a zip code where 42.9 percent of residents have less than a ninth-grade education. One conclusion: these Music & Youth Development Alliance member organizations are important, stable, and lasting engines of change in their community.

In some cases, your campaign can succeed, and you still fail. A good example of learning from failure comes particularly to mind: the website of one of our clients was incomprehensible, and as a result, they had no follow-up mechanisms in place to engage people who landed on their site. No matter how many people the Influencer Effect drove to it, nothing more happened. This situation was frustrating, but our reporting to the client referenced this. They instigated an overhaul of their website, and subsequent campaigns did far better.

While there are few downsides to measurement, there certainly can be frustrations. These include the time and challenges of getting quality data at a reasonable cost. However, if you are thoughtful, intentional, and persistent, you can get the information you need to show how your campaign performed.

Presenting Your Findings

Go on the road, internally and externally, to show what emerged from your measurement. Take the results and ask, "Did the people that matter feel satisfied with the outcome?"

Disseminating your data to stakeholders cohesively and appealingly matters almost as much as its content. By communicating well, you can move your organization forward. Below are a few things to keep in mind when presenting your data.

Tell Stories

Fundamentally, measurement tells stories and that is what leads to change. We all relate to stories, so fill your stakeholders' heads with facts and their hearts with emotion. ALIMA US's campaign raised $4 million to buy oxygenators (tactical impact), which resulted in a 6 percent decrease in West African COVID-19 deaths (ultimate impact). These hard facts show that the programs are working. If you then couple this statistic with a video of a mother and her children celebrating her husband's recovery, the story has a resonance beyond statistics. We love stories, so use your data to tell emotional stories. Satisfy both the heart and the head.

Which Data

How do you choose which data to share to tell your success stories? Let's suppose you have two data sets to work with. One is a case study: a Year Up graduate, formerly living in a homeless shelter, now has a full-time job and an apartment. The second shows that the percentage of leads to Year Up's website grew over the campaign period by 27.6 percent, and this month, youth enrollment in the program grew by 15 percent compared to last month. The former resonates with young people who are potential applicants to the program and the latter with foundations and future employers. Use both, but for different audiences.

It is important to ask yourself continually, "Who is my audience?" Age, language, education, and culture will inform both the form and substance of your presentation. If English is a second language for your audience, don't use slang or complex words.

> ***Pro Tip:*** *Most people don't remember numbers, especially if you have lots of them, so always put your numbers in context and relate them to a finding that people will remember. When providing data for public consumption, rather than saying 21.33% of males ages 13 to 19 years suffer from at least one diagnosable mental health disorder, state that approximately one in five teens suffer from mental health issues.*

The Format

Are you using PowerPoint, a pdf, a document, or a video? Consider which method will be best for your recipient. Your public-facing platforms such as your website, email list, magazines, YouTube channel, and social channels are all ways to disseminate your findings to the world.

Visuals

You can represent your data in various ways, from bar graphs to pie charts. The Influencer Effect often manifests through social media, so if you have a screenshot of a Tweet or an Instagram or TikTok post, show this in your presentation. Most people respond better to visuals, and to video in particular.

One of my favorite ways to report information is through infographics, which is a visual, succinct representation of your data and results. You can use infographics before, during, and after your campaign, in real-time if needed. I also love a good dashboard as it is a visible, informative, and straightforward way to show your KPIs over a specific period.

> **Pro Tip:** *Whether you present your findings in person or video conference, not every decision maker will attend a meeting, so always have a self-explanatory leave-behind document.*

Length

British Prime Minister and logophile Winston Churchill said, "This report by its very length, defends itself from the risk of being read." If your CEO runs from meeting to meeting, then a thirty-page report is not the way to go. Instead, they will benefit from an executive summary. At the same time, a more comprehensive case study or a peer-reviewed academic paper on behavior change and the Influencer Effect may work well for those studying it in-depth.

Wrap Report

At the end of each campaign, I create a wrap report for clients and internal use. This sets out the campaign's story and has a "Lessons Learned" section that contains positive and negative outcomes. Often I have successes and failures within the same campaign. The wrap report is one of my most valuable feedback tools. We all learn from the data, even if it shows failure alongside triumph. If your campaign doesn't, you are fooling yourself. From the lessons learned, you can calibrate your approach to the future.

To sum up, you can measure the Influencer Effect in concrete ways that convincingly demonstrate the positives achieved and give meaning to your campaign. This information allows you to drive your organization, cause, and business forward. The benefits of measuring far outweigh the effort, so please become a measurer.

CHAPTER 7

MAKE YOUR D.R.E.A.M. A REALITY

Don't dream it, be it!

TIM CURRY, "DON'T DREAM IT"
FROM *THE ROCKY HORROR PICTURE SHOW*

Y<small>OU FOLLOWED THE</small> D.R.E.A.M. <small>METHOD</small> and evoked the Influencer Effect. Congratulations, you will now be looking back at a successful campaign. You will also be looking forward to your next one with more experience, resources, and confidence.

However, if you have just read this book for the first time and have yet to implement the D.R.E.A.M. method, you may be feeling that you have an abundance of information to absorb and apply. You are right. I have downloaded decades of experience for you, but in tasty bite-size morsels to make absorption and application simple.

These are the five most common reasons the Influencer Effect fails:

- Not starting in the first place.
- Not allowing enough time to plan and execute.
- Not defining and measuring your goals.
- Not casting a wide enough Influencer net.
- Not executing professionally.

This book is structured to make it easy for you to go back and reference any specific part of the D.R.E.A.M. method at any time during your campaign. I am also available to answer questions at info@goodinfluencebook.com.

The D.R.E.A.M. method consists of five manageable steps, and within each step, specific actions to take. My recommendation is to start to DESIGN YOUR ACTION PLAN. With your direction set, you will have clarity and certainty. From there, RESEARCH the right Influencers for your campaign. Having chosen your Influencers, ENGAGE them. You are now all set to ACTIVATE your campaign and MEASURE the benefits from your Influencer Effect.

The Influencer Effect will raise awareness, support, and revenues, inspire action and advocacy, and propel your programs. It is an exponentially powerful attractor and amplifier, especially when an Influencer, brand, and nonprofit combine in a Multi-Pact. Whether your goals are purpose, profit, or both, the Influencer Effect will get you well beyond the finish line.

Each campaign is different and can be unpredictable. To me, that's exciting. However, the best practices and guidelines set out in this book will give you predictable and measurable methods to invoke. One of my goals is for the stories, information, and good vibes you find in *Good Influence* to give you the confidence and the knowledge you need to move forward.

As you have undoubtedly gathered, my main focus is on the Influencer Effect being employed for good. By working with Influencers, you will become an enlightened and savvy business that is part of the rapidly growing field that I named "Cause Influence."

Cause Influence is where Influencers, entertainment properties, and popular culture's influence, knowledge, and cultural capital is engaged to advance social and philanthropic causes. Cause Influence harnesses this power for purpose and profit. The analogous cause marketing industry generates revenues in excess of $2.2 billion a year. The exploding field of "Cause Influence," powered by the Influencer Effect and utilizing the Multi-Pact model, which fits nicely under the $14 Billion a year general Influencer marketing banner, can imitate, replicate, and possibly exceed that amount. Despite being a fast-growing industry sector, Cause Influence holds vast potential for even more good to be unleashed by organizations of all shapes and sizes. Cause Influence needs to be a strategic priority for every for-profit and nonprofit with dedicated resources and focus. And, yes, this still holds true even if your Influencer is a Pomeranian dog called Jiff Pom.

Both Airbnb and the Taproot Foundation bring together interested parties for their mutual benefit. In Airbnb's case, property owners with travelers, and in Taproot, skilled corporate volunteers to support nonprofits. Cause Influence

aims, in part, to be a similar catalyst for Influencers, businesses, and nonprofits to come together for social good on
a grander scale.

   To strengthen the field of Cause Influence, I am continually introducing best practices, creating knowledge bases, and
strengthening networks with aligned academic, philanthropic,
and business partners. Over the coming years and beyond,
I hope that Cause Influence continues to build momentum,
inspire others to join, create economic opportunity, and most
importantly, contribute to a better world for us all. My philosophy has always been one of open architecture, sharing
ideas, and getting more people involved. We can create the
most good for the maximum number of people by working
together. Whether it's me that does the work or others is not
relevant. That it happens is what matters.

   Please regularly check out goodinfluencebook.com for
updates, tools, forms, and case studies. Think of it as the
Consumer Reports of Cause Influence. Know that I am here
to help and support you, so don't hesitate to contact me.

What Can You Do Now?

Whether you are at a company or nonprofit, use this book to
engage Influencers and employ the Influencer Effect. If you
are an Influencer, get involved in a cause that you believe in.
Hopefully, the three of you can come together in a Multi-Pact
to maximize your effectiveness and karma.

I want to make a special appeal to those younger celebrities, athletes, and social media influencers to dedicate part of your activities to philanthropy and social justice rather than only focusing on fame and money. Some already do this, but more can join the ranks of Influencers doing good. You will find this pursuit is not only immensely rewarding but that it also adds longevity to your career and happiness to your life. Perhaps you have a cause you care about that needs urgent attention. Use your Influencer Effect to benefit yourself, your organization, and our interconnected world.

To me, the only way to fail is not to start. By taking your first step, you will go on your own incredible and illuminating journey. This adventure will culminate in the successes you deserve, and you'll benefit others along the way. Ultimately, what better purpose and outcome in life is there than doing good.

MUSIC LYRIC ACKNOWLEDGMENTS

Chapter 1: "O Day"
Words and Music by Robert Diggs Jr.
Copyright © 2008 by Universal Music – Careers and Ramecca
    Publishing All Rights Administered by Universal Music
    – Careers
International Copyright Secured. All Rights Reserved
Reprinted by Permission of Hal Leonard LLC

Chapter 2: "No Surprises"
Words and Music by COLIN GREENWOOD, JONATHAN
    GREENWOOD, EDWARD O'BRIEN, PHILIP SELWAY
    and THOMAS YORKE
© 1997 WARNER CHAPPELL MUSIC LTD.
All Rights in the U.S. and Canada Administered by WC
    MUSIC CORP. All Rights Reserved
Used by Permission of ALFRED MUSIC

Chapter 3: "B.I.B.L.E. (Basic Instructions Before Leaving Earth)"

Words and Music by Gary Grice and Robert Diggs
Copyright © 1995 UNIVERSAL – POLYGRAM INTERNA-
   TIONAL PUBLISHING, INC., GZA MUSIC PUBLISHING,
   UNIVERSAL MUSIC – CAREERS and RAMECCA
   PUBLISHING, INC.
All Rights for GZA MUSIC PUBLISHING Administered
   by UNIVERSAL – POLYGRAM INTERNATIONAL
   PUBLISHING, INC.
All Rights for RAMECCA PUBLISHING, INC. Administered
   by UNIVERSAL MUSIC – CAREERS
All Rights Reserved. Used by Permission
Reprinted by Permission of Hal Leonard LLC

"Real"

Words and Music by Kendrick Lamar, Terrace Martin and
   Marlon Williams
© 2012 WC MUSIC CORP., HARD WORKING BLACK FOLKS
   INC., TOP DAWG MUSIC, MUSIC OF WINDSWEPT,
   ROSEMAC MUSIC and ROYNET MUSIC
All Rights for HARD WORKING BLACK FOLKS INC. and
   TOP DAWG MUSIC Administered by WC MUSIC CORP.
All Rights for MUSIC OF WINDSWEPT and ROSEMAC
   MUSIC Administered by BMG RIGHTS MANAGEMENT
   (US) LLC
All Rights Reserved. Used by Permission
Reprinted by Permission of Hal Leonard LLC

Chapter 4: "Confusion is Next"

Words and music by Kim Gordon, Thurston Moore, Lee Ranaldo, and James Sclavno

© 1983 Sonik Tooth Publishing

All Rights of Sonik Tooth Publishing for Kim Gordon, Thurston Moore, and Lee Ranaldo.

Administered by Songs of Kobalt Music Publishing, and for James Sclavno administered by Sentric Music Publishing Limited

All Rights Reserved. Used by Permission

Chapter 5: "Texan Love Song"

Words by Bernie Taupin

Music by Elton John

Copyright © 1972 UNIVERSAL/DICK JAMES MUSIC LTD.

Copyright Renewed

All Rights in the United States Administered by UNIVERSAL – SONGS OF POLYGRAM INTERNATIONAL, INC.

All Rights Reserved Used by Permission

Chapter 6: "Boss"

Words and Music by Beyonce Knowles, Shawn Carter, Dernest Emile and Tyrone Griffin Jr.

Copyright © 2018 Oakland 13 Music, Carter Boys Music, BMG Platinum Songs US, DII Music LLC, Tailored 4U Music LLC, These Are Pulse Songs and UP10M's Publishing

All Rights on behalf of Oakland 13 Music and Carter Boys Music Administered by Sony Music Publishing (US) LLC, 424 Church Street, Suite 1200, Nashville, TN 37219

Chapter 7: "Don't Dream It, Be It"

BIBLIOGRAPHY

Allison + Partners. "Allison + Partners' New Influence Impact Study Shows Digital Influencers Drive Donations And Engagement with Causes." *Allison+Partners* (blog). June 26, 2017. Accessed March 15, 2022. https://www.allisonpr.com/blog/allisonpartners-new-influence-impact-study-shows-digital-influencers-drive-donations-and-engagement-with-causes/

Banister, EN, and HL Cocker, "A cultural exploration of consumers' interactions and relationships with celebrities." *Journal of Marketing Management* (2014).

Blakley, Johanna, Adam Amel Rogers, Erica Watson-Currie, and Kristin (Eun Jung) Jung. "Africa in the Media." *University of Southern California's Norman Lear Center* (website). January 2019. Accessed March 30, 2022. http://www.mediaimpactproject.org/uploads/5/1/2/7/5127770/africainthemedia2019.pdf

BOOSTO. "Businesses Use Influencer Marketing to Lift Brand Recall." *Medium* (blog). May 14, 2019. Accessed February 23, 2022. https://medium.com/boosto/businesses-use-influencer-marketing-to-lift-brand-recall-12181695ab79

Charm, Tamara, Janette Hwang, Jackie Laird, Nancy Lu, Jason Rico Saavedra, Andrea Leon, Daniela Sancho Mazzara, Anirvan Maiti, Kelsey Robinson, and Tom Skiles. "US Consumer Sentiment and

Behaviors During the Coronavirus Crisis." *McKinsey* (website). December 14, 2021. Accessed February 22, 2022. https://www.mckinsey.com/business-functions/marketing-and-sales/our-insights/survey-us-consumer-sentiment-during-the-coronavirus-crisis

Christensen, Clayton M., Scott Cook, and Taddy Hall. "Marketing Malpractice: The Cause and the Cure." *The Harvard Business Review Magazine*. (December 2005).

Ciotti, Gregory. "Understanding Consumer Behavior to Convert More Customers." *Help Scout* (website). Accessed February 24, 2022. https://www.helpscout.com/consumer-behavior/

Digital Marketing Institute. "20 Surprising Influencer Marketing Statistics." *Digital Marketing Institute* (website). October 19, 2021. Accessed March 15, 2022. https://digitalmarketinginstitute.com/blog/20-influencer-marketing-statistics-that-will-surprise-you

Duthie, Elizabeth, Diogo Verissimo, Aidan Keane, and Andrew T. Knight. "The Effectiveness of Celebrities in Conservation Marketing." *Plos One* 12, no.7 (July 2017). https://doi.org/10.1371/journal.pone.0180027

Elberse, Anita, and Jeroen Verleun. 2012. "The Economic Value of Celebrity Endorsements." *Journal of Advertising Research* 52, no 2 (June 2012): 149-165. https://doi.org/10.2501/JAR-52-2-149-165

Fein, David, Samuel Dastrup, and Kimberly Burnett. "Still Bridging the Opportunity Divide for Low-Income Youth: Year Up's Longer-Term Impacts." *Administration for Children and Families*. April 2021. Accessed March 30, 2022. https://www.acf.hhs.gov/sites/default/files/documents/opre/year-up-report-april-2021.pdf

Harris, Erica E., and Julie A. Ruth. "Analysis of the Value of Celebrity Affiliation to Nonprofit Contributions." *Nonprofit and Voluntary Sector Quarterly* 44, no 5 (September 2014): 945-967. https://doi.org/10.1177/0899764014546428

Hofmann, Karen, and Deepika Malhotra. "Pervasive Analytics: Measuring the Impact of a Celebrity Direct-to-Customer Campaign in Pharma." *Cognizant* (website). September 2015. https://www.cognizant.com/us/en/archives/whitepapers/documents/Pervasive-Analytics-Measuring-the-Impact-of-a-Celebrity-Direct-to-Customer-Campaign-in-Pharma-codex1415.pdf

Insights Association. "Code of Standards and Ethics for Market Research and Data Analytics." *Insights Association*. November 2021. Accessed March 30, 2022. https://www.insightsassociation.org/Portals/INSIGHTS/ia_code_revised_november_2021_finalv2.pdf

Institute for Public Relations. "About Public Relations Research Standards Center (PRRSC)." *Institute for Public Relations* (organization website). Accessed February 24, 2022. https://instituteforpr.org/public-relations-research-standards/about/

Ismail, Kaya. "Social Media Influencers: Mega, Macro, Micro or Nano." *CMS WiRE* (website). December 10, 2018. https://www.cmswire.com/digital-marketing/social-media-influencers-mega-macro-micro-or-nano/

Kamins, Michael A., and Kamal Gupta. "Congruence between Spokesperson and Product Type: A Matchup Hypothesis Perspective." *Psychology & Marketing* (Wiley) 11, no 6 (November 1994): 569-586.

Kaplowitz, Rella. "Data Playbook." *The Charles and Lynn Schusterman Family Foundation*. Accessed March 30, 2022. https://www.schusterman.org/playbooks/data/files/Data_Playbook_Final.pdf

Kaufman, Gil. "Study Claims Logic's '1-800-273-8255' Anthem Saved Hundreds of Lives." *Billboard* (website). December 14, 2021. https://www.billboard.com/music/rb-hip-hop/logic-1-800-song-saved-lives-suicide-report-1235010081/

Klien, Jessica. "38% Of Gen Z And Millennials Trust Digital Influencers, Says Fullscreen Study." Tubefilter.

March 27, 2018. https://www.tubefilter.com/2018/03/27/gen-z-millennials-trust-influencers-fullscreen/

Lawson-Zilai, Lauren. "Cause Docs: Lauren Lawson-Zilai, Goodwill Industries International." *The Doctor is In.* Hosted by Joe Waters. June 3, 2021. https://lu.ma/influencer-marketing

Levitt, Steven D. "So Much for One Person, One Vote." *The New York Times.* August 6, 2008.

McKinsey & Company. "Perspectives on Retail and Consumer Goods." *McKinsey & Company,* no 8 (August 2020).

Morain, Claudia. "Tiger Woods Scandal Cost Shareholders up to $12 Billion." *UC Davis* (website). December 28, 2009. Accessed March 15, 2022. https://www.ucdavis.edu/news/tiger-woods-scandal-cost-shareholders-12-billion

Moulard, Julie Guidry, Carolyn Popp Garrity, and Dan Hamilton Rice. "What Makes a Human Brand Authentic? Identifying the Antecedents of Celebrity Authenticity." *Psychology & Marketing* 32, no. 2 (January 14, 2015): 173-186. https://doi.org/10.1002/mar.20771

Murray, Rheana. "Subway Commercial Spokesman Jared Fogle Marks 15 Years of Turkey Subs and Keeping the Weight Off." *New York Daily News.* June 9, 2013. Accessed February 22, 2022. https://www.nydailynews.com/life-style/health/jared-subway-guy-marks-15-years-turkey-subs-article-1.1365511

Nielsen Company. "Global Trust in Advertising: Winning Strategies for an Evolving Media Landscape." *Nielsen.* September 2015. Accessed February 22, 2022. https://www.nielsen.com/wp-content/uploads/sites/3/2019/04/global-trust-in-advertising-report-sept-2015-1.pdf

Raedts, Maddie. "Five Ways to Create Effective Conversion-Driven Influencer Campaigns." *Forbes.* July 12, 2019.

https://www.forbes.com/sites/forbesagencycouncil/2019/07/12/five-ways-to-create-effective-conversion-driven-influencer-campaigns/?sh=32dfe34745e9

Rosen, Yereth. "Bristol Palin Earned $262,500 from Sex Abstinence Work." *Reuters.* April 5, 2011. https://www.reuters.com/article/us-palin-earnings/bristol-palin-earned-262500-from-sex-abstinence-work-idUSTRE7347T220110405

Saint, Benjy. "Why Celebrity Endorsements are Still Essential to Charities." *nfpSynergy* (website). August 22, 2019. Accessed February 09, 2022. https://nfpsynergy.net/blog/why-celebrity-endorsements-are-still-essential-charities

Saleh, Khalid. "The Average Website Conversion Rate by Industry." *Invesp.* Accessed February 24, 2022. https://www.invespcro.com/blog/the-average-website-conversion-rate-by-industry/

Seattle Software Developers. "Most Overused Celebrities of the Past Decade." *Seattle Software Developers* (website). January 15, 2021. https://seattlesoftwaredevelopers.com/overused-celebrities/

Sharpe Group. "12 Interesting Fundraising Statistics Everyone Should Know." *Sharpe Group* (website). Accessed February 22, 2022. https://sharpenet.com/interesting-fundraising-statistics-everyone-should-know/

Sheffield, Matthew. "Poll: Most Voters Say Celebrity Political Endorsements Don't Matter." *The Hill.* June 14, 2019. Accessed February 24, 2022. https://thehill.com/hilltv/what-americas-thinking/448585-poll-most-americans-say-celebrity-political-endorsements-have

Social Value International. "Principles of Social Value." *Social Value International.* Accessed March 30, 2022. https://static1.squarespace.com/static/60dc51e3c58aef413ae5c975/t/6127b55936e97e03e86297ea/1629992289441/Principles+of+Social+Value+.pdf

Takumi. "The Realities of Influencer Marketing: TikTok and YouTube in Focus." (whitepaper). *Takumi*. May 2020.

Tomoson. "Influencer Marketing Study." *Tomoson*. Accessed February 23, 2022. https://www.tomoson.com/blog/influencer-marketing-study/

Veer, Ekant, Ilda Becirovic, and Brett AS Martin. "If Kate Voted Conservative, Would You? The Role of Celebrity Endorsements in Political Party Advertising." *European Journal of Marketing* 44, no. 3 (April 2010): 436-450. https://doi.org/10.1108/03090561011020516

Wong, Vanessa. "Subway Sales Keep Falling in 2015." *BuzzFeed News*. March 29, 2016. Accessed February 22, 2022. https://www.buzzfeednews.com/article/venessawong/subway-sales-kept-falling-in-2015#.xbqpZbDwX

Yermack, David. "Vision Statement: How This First Lady Moves Markets." *Harvard Business Review*. November 2010. https://hbr.org/2010/11/vision-statement-how-this-first-lady-moves-markets

Zhang, Lu, and Wei Wei. "Influencer Marketing: A Comparison of Traditional Celebrity, Social Media Influencer, and AI Influencer." *Boston Hospitality Review*. October 4, 2021. https://www.bu.edu/bhr/2021/10/04/influencer-marketing-a-comparison-of-tradi-tional-celebrity-social-media-influencer-and-ai-influencer/

INDEX